MW01487995

Confessions of a
MAN
Evolution of a PLAYA

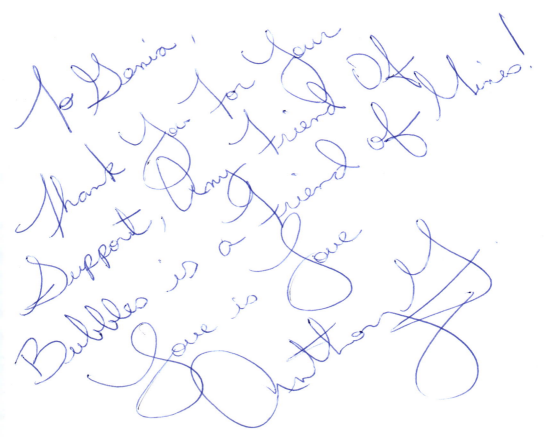

To Genia,

Thank You for Your
support, Amy friend of
Bubbles is a friend
of Mine!

Love is Love

Anthony

Confessions of a MAN
Evolution of a Playa

Published by In the Trenches
www.inthetrenches.com
© 2016 Anthony Jae Gonzalez

All rights reserved. No part of this publication may be reproduced, distributed, or transmitted in any form or by any means, including photocopying, recording, or other electronic or mechanical methods, without the prior written permission of the publisher, except in the case of brief quotations embodied in critical reviews and certain other noncommercial uses permitted by copyright law.

ISBN: 978-0-9981865-2-8

Cover and page design by Toelke Associates
www.toelkeassociates.com

Photographer: "Live Thru Love," Tmari30112@gmail.com

Proofreaders/Editors:
Denise Moore: ddb2475@gmail.com
Erika Melanie: erika.riddick@gmail.com
Sarah Lovell: steal337@gmail.com

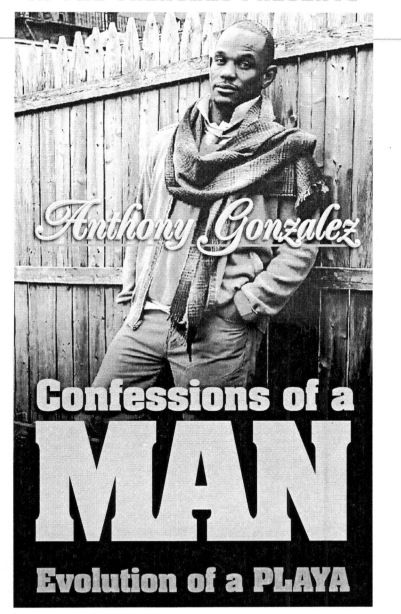

Contents

Acknowledgements   vi

Prologue   viii

Confession 1   1

Virgin Island '83–'84   4

Confession 2   9

Bedroom Bully '91   13

Be All You Can Be '96–'97   18

Confession 3   24

Clueless '92   29

Ready or Not Part One '93   33

Confession 4   37

The Boy Is Mine '93–'94   41

Great Adventures '93 & '01   48

Confession 5   55

Early Morning Wake Up '98–'99   60

False Hope '04–'05   68

   Confession 6   72

Blind Date '00   75

Icy & Hot   84

All in the Family   94

   Confession 7   108

Hit & Run '00–'01   111

Can I Have Some? '06   122

The Breakdown   131

Ready or Not Part Two '04–'05   136

About the Author   138

Acknowledgments

They say that it takes a village to raise a child, so with that being said ... I'd like to thank my entire village: The Hunter/Newton Family, The Otero/Gonzalez Family, The Roman/Rosario Family, The Ortiz/Velez/Davila/Reyes Family, The Jordan/Gregg Family, all of which play a significant part in my upbringing in one way or another. I wouldn't be the man that I am if not for my village, love y'all to the death of me and beyond.

I'd also like to thank my Cozine/Workman/Pink Houses & Newlots Brothers and Sisters. Y'all know who y'all are and make no mistake about it I mean brother and sisters literally.

Much thanks goes to my son, Dominic C. Taylor 'cause if not him I wouldn't have entertained the idea of writing books. The first book I wrote wasn't this one, it was what I consider a book of enlightenment which was inspired by him. Soon to be released...

A special thanks goes to my Team — aka Family — Denise Moore, Tanya M. Smith, Erika Melanie, Carol Sheffer, and Sarah Lovell. These women each believed enough in me and this book to dedicate themselves to the making of it. If not for them, I can honestly say that this book would have still been in manuscript (hand written) form and somewhere in a manila envelope.

I can't forget the haters, the fakes, and the snakes 'cause you too played a part in who I've become. Thank y'all and rest assured I know who you all are, Smfh/Lmfao... ..

Thanks also goes to all of the females I've crossed paths with because you too played a part in the man I've become... .

Anthony Jae Gonzalez

Prologue

This book has been put together in an informative, yet entertaining, format. It is based on actual events, facts, and emotions that I have experienced. Out of respect, I have altered the names of the people I mention. This book is composed of my innermost feelings and thoughts about my sexual experiences. I do not mean to offend any particular gender and/or race. My apologies go out in advance if I do so.

It took me years to actually understand the renowned word "playa." A playa has many advantages and disadvantages depending on where one stands in life. My intention is to enlighten people on those advantages and disadvantages from where I stood and now stand. I have come to believe that a true playa is a pimp in training. Also, that a true playa's love is actually lust. If he claims otherwise, he is simply playing along. Eventually, one will realize they're playing themselves and stop playing this game if they ever want a chance of having a meaningful relationship with one person. There comes a time when a person must realize that a true playa loves no one but themselves.

Anybody could be considered a playa. By that I mean a playboy, a gigolo, a womanizer, or a john. Even a female can be considered a playa, although it's not respected due to their gender. Yet, for women, it mainly depends on their habits and actions. Whether one respects the game or not, who decides who's the playa haters and the playas?

A true playa is in fact up front about his position to avoid any misunderstandings and/or drama. Nobody has the right to claim to be a playa if they are in a relationship. If so, then that so called "playa" isn't nothing more than a cheater and/or adulteress. There are rules to everything; being a womanizer, playboy, gigolo, pimp, john, or the so called "playa." Once a person doesn't follow the rules in any way, they must evaluate their position in the game and in life.

Back then I was left with the wrong impression of what females expected from me. It took a long time before I realized what I was supposed to do, and what I was expected to do in order to have a good woman.

THESE ARE MY CONFESSIONS

Confession 1

My first sexual experience had my nose wide open. I just wanted to have sex every chance I got and I never wanted the relationship to end. The funny thing was that other than the times we were fucking, she acted like I didn't exist. It fucked me up because when we were together we would have sex every available moment. Outside of the room, I was just a boy she knew from the hood. We both were very young, so I understand why it was a "behind closed doors" relationship. We didn't have any business being naked like that in the first place, curiosity killed the cat. Things were like that between us for a long time and then one day she was gone. Her family had moved and I felt sick because I didn't want her to go away.

I really liked Veronica even though she was younger than me. It may just have been lust. I was addicted to her and what she opened my eyes to. I probably would've done anything she wanted just for some of her loving. I think the only person who had an idea about us was my uncle. Still, he never explained much to me about what is known as, "The birds and the bees." I found it all out on my own as I got older and had more sexual experiences with different types of women. This was enlightening. Growing up, I witnessed and heard a lot due to all the hookers that passed through my house, as well as my experiences with Veronica. I believed everything was just about sex. As time went on, my only motive with the females I messed with was sex.

As a kid, I never thought that emotions had to be involved in a relationship in order for it to be meaningful. This idea blew up in my face as the years went on and I tried to figure women out. I came close a few times, got lucky once in a while, but my fingers had more pleasure than me. It soon became evident that getting pussy meant agreeing to a relationship.

I had no problem with that, as long as I got some sex out of it. I could care less what they thought about me because I didn't have many real feelings for them. I just wanted to fuck and move on. Emotional feelings were never really a factor. My focus was on the feelings I received whenever they provided me with sexual favors. That was the only pleasure I cared for and desired. I would say and/or agree to just about anything just to have sex with a female. There were quite a few that I assumed wanted me to be committed, yet my commitment varied greatly from theirs. Most realized that later down the line when I felt the need to move on to the next female.

I let down these females the same way my first crush let me down. I thought that's how you were supposed to end relationships. I didn't know any better and nobody ever told me there was a formal way to do so. At that time, it wasn't like I cared away. Now, I've learned this is absolutely not the case.

I would just leave without saying good-bye. It always seemed that when I did commit, I got let down or was disappointed somehow. So, in my eyes, I was doing the same thing to them because I felt it was only right in all fairness.

Still I had to learn all about women on my own and from others with self-proclaimed knowledge. With all that being said, a playa was born and I began to play along with the playas. I followed in the footsteps of those who I thought knew better and only later on down the line did I learn otherwise.

This is all I knew for a long time and that's how all my female encounters were. I was playing them.

Virgin Island
'83-'84

I lost my virginity to a girl named Veronica. I was probably about eleven years old. She was a young, sexy Latina I used to babysit when our parents went out. They frequented the bar and clubs. While they were out partying, we were home alone. Veronica was a year or two younger than me, but her actions and ways would have you believe otherwise. To be completely honest, I truly doubt she was even a virgin at the time. She was far too boy friendly to be inexperienced. She had long, dark black hair, a butterscotch complexion, and some chinky eyes. I can't forget the fact that she had a pretty smile. One day after school, while our parents were at work, Veronica's sister asked me if Veronica could stay with me until she finished running some errands. That was like music to my ears. I was quick to say yes and shortly thereafter, Veronica came over.

Our parents weren't due back home until 5 o'clock that evening. So we took it upon ourselves to play house and since I was already watching my siblings, Veronica and I played the role of parents. I was the husband not thinking I was going to be doing all the "husband" duties. I shared a room with my sister and younger brothers. It was a big two family flat. So it wasn't hard to find privacy in our house and Veronica being the "mother," made sure we had privacy to play our little game. She had the other kids do their homework and then watch some T.V., while having me wait for her in the bedroom. She was obviously running the show.

Our room was set up with bunk beds on one side, a dresser in between the beds, one being on each end and a twin bed on the other side of the room. I took it upon myself to hang a sheet from the top bunk; that way it would make the bottom bunk more like a tent for our private moment. When she appeared in the room she was smiling and had this curious look on her face. I figured we were going to kiss and pretend to have sex. I was going to do whatever she wanted, taking complete advantage of being alone with her. This was already more than I expected from Veronica and I was not going to mess it up. I was happy that I was going to get to kiss her.

As soon as we slid onto the bottom bunk we were full of smiles and giggles. It was light outside yet the sheet caused a darker illusion for my homemade tent. Veronica then looked at me with a not-so-innocent look and said, "Take off your clothes." A surprised but shocked look crossed my face for a brief moment. I thought she was playing a joke. I didn't quite understand what she had requested. That was until she began taking off her clothes right in front of me. I realized she wasn't playing. At this point, I had no clue what was about to go down.

After all our clothes were off, she laid down and called for me to climb on top of her. I did as I was told and asked, "What about the kids?" Veronica quickly responded, "Don't worry. They won't bother us."

With that being said, I began to nervously kiss Veronica and she began to hump me while holding onto my waist. At 9 years old, how did she know how to do this? I got excited and I enjoyed the benefits of being the "husband." It was not long before the humping stopped and her hand was on my dick. I thought she was just going to stroke it or something. Once again, I was clueless as to what was going on until I felt my dick sliding into her. I was amazed at the way I suddenly was feeling. Every thrust sent warm sensations through my body. It was then that I realized having sex was completely different from grinding on each other. I felt this wetness around my dick that I couldn't explain. I slipped out a couple of times until we adjusted to one another. I didn't want this to ever come to an end. I was enjoying all of it way too much.

While we were having sex, at that point with a better understanding of what we were doing, I noticed the hanging sheet move slightly. I instantly got nervous, not knowing who it was. That's when my brother's face appeared. I told myself relax. I had to stop pumping her hairless vagina, and demanded that he go play somewhere else. He was messing up my flow. I was really starting to get into it because I found my rhythm. He just stared with this blank look on his face and was reluctant to leave, almost like he was interested. Although I was upset he had interrupted, I refused to pull my dick from inside of her. Veronica, on the other hand, found him and his behavior cute. She politely asked me to move for a minute as she turned to pick up my brother. Did this girl not know what we were doing? Did she realize that I was having the time of my life and it was abruptly ended by my nosey brother?

Veronica saw the disappointment in my face and I became furious with my little brother. I sat back as he was lifted on top of her naked body and she rocked him back and forth in her lap. He was wearing nothing but his underwear, which she took upon herself to pull down a little bit. She laid back and calmed him by allowing him to rub his little parts on her. I was amazed at what she was doing. I caught myself feeling jealous. I was getting annoyed. I wanted Veronica all to myself, especially since she taught me what sex really was.

I needed to know more, so I'd know what to do next. I was trying to find out as much as possible in a short amount of time. We were racing against the clock because our parents would be coming back soon. After awhile, which felt like forever, she removed him from on top of her, placing him back on the floor. With his underwear back on fully, she told him to go play. Just like that, he was gone. I was mesmerized by how fast he was out of the room and I quickly resumed my position on top of Veronica.

This time, I directed my dick back inside of her vagina myself. I pumped for a little while longer. We knew we had to stop before any adults came in. From that day forth, every time I got a chance to babysit for her mother or sister… I would! Each and every time we would fuck like animals. Come to find out, Veronica was molested at a very young age and she thought that what we were doing was a normal thing for a young girl to do. These are the types of things that happen and have women twisted later in life. Without some kind of therapy, they end up running into the arms of men that are no good; thinking that they are the best thing for them. Without that knowledge of what to expect from a man, you will end up with the lowest of the low. Unbeknownst to women who don't know what to look for or are brainwashed into thinking that these types of "men" love them, they are the WORST ones possible for them. Here we go with the self-esteem issues, and emotional breakdowns that women suffer from and want another man to understand what they been through and to put up with it.

In the end, women lose out on a potentially good man because of their insecurities and trust issues. Veronica moved and I never saw her again.

Confession 2

used to believe that I was a sex fiend. I couldn't get enough. Then I met these two particular females. They knew what they wanted and made sure they received it. With each of these experiences, both females truly were sex fanatics. Before my encounters with these two, I thought I knew women. At that time, there weren't any females that I couldn't handle. These two women proved that I shouldn't judge a book by its cover because inside, each book showed me a whole different story. I was a compliant participant and I didn't have control over anything that happened during each of these encounters. I didn't like either female enough to be in a relationship, but I thought they were good enough to sleep with and get what I needed. They both were very independent and preferred not to commit to any relationships. They both expressed similar ideas about mono-gamy being a conflict of interest. I didn't have time for a relationship anyway. I was on some real promiscuous, "I need to try some of everyone" shit. They both had been through something in previous relationships that ultimately hindered their view of "normal" rela-tionships. They had their own rules they wanted to play by.

These women were just enjoying the moments because they didn't have time to get caught up in feelings. I was happy to know that I wasn't the only one who thought that way. Only a few select females were satisfied with not being sexually involved without the burden of a commitment. I have learned to respect women, as well as their decisions, without treating them any less.

It's not fair to consider a female less of a woman because she chooses to be promiscuous. I had a newfound respect for women who took charge or liked to be in control sexually. They "get theirs" and be gone, allowing no time for pillow talk. A little small talk was considered okay, although not always necessary.

Now at this point, I was in my early to mid-twenties. Tatiana was twenty and a bit more than I had expected at the time. I was astonished at how long she would like to spend having or demand-ing sex. I have to admit, she brought the best out of me and refused to accept anything less. She groomed me; taught me to be aggres-sive and how to dominate the pussy. However, just to be clear, this aggressive behavior isn't for everyone. Also, if one chooses to be promiscuous, there is no time for love making. In other words, no philandering. Tatiana knew what she wanted, set out to get it, and then went on her way. Before having sex with Tatiana, I really didn't know any girl who could manhandle me in bed. To be completely honest, I used to think I was too much to handle. I surely learned that was not the case.

In fact, I can admit that she taught me a few things. When this female named Chastity came into the picture, I was more experienced in bed.

She was about to go to the army (boot camp) and wanted to get wild before she left. She, too, was unrestrained. She took pride in that. Chastity was also determined to make something positive of her life by any means necessary. In a way, she felt unshackled and refused to let anybody rob her of that. I respected her for that. In fact, I envied her because I knew nothing about feeling set free. I was honored to be the one she wanted to have crazy, hot, sweaty sex with before she left. I have to admit that although we were no strangers in this department, she definitely out did herself on that one particular occasion before she left.

I have learned a lot about promiscuous women and about what is expected of the men they deal with. One thing is that they openly admit they have numerous sexual partners on a casual basis and aren't willing to easily compromise. I also realized that it takes a strong woman to have multiple partners and demand respect. These days, one man is not enough for many of these females. I guess everybody has a purpose.

I, for one, have a lot of respect for promiscuous people as long as they have their priorities in order. I also learned that most of the men these females deal with try to take away their freedom. There are a lot of men who truly can't handle or won't accept a strong, liberated woman. Men often look to possess and control them. Meanwhile, they are sleeping around with a bunch of different women. They lack the ability to deal with strong-minded, free-willed women. I believe if men could accept and appreciate independent women, while taking the time to truly understand what that means, we would all get along so much better and be more open to faithfulness.

It will always be hard for a man to accept a woman that is independent, educated, intelligent, strong-minded and free willed, because she doesn't have to depend on him. That's what a lot of men look for, but then use as ammo against them later. It will always be a problem for a man to accept a woman with that playa mentality because it means she will be able like he treats her; "when I am done with you, be gone."

Tatiana and Chastity taught me to be upfront about being promiscuous and not worry about being in a one woman relationship. Whether some people know it or not, being in a monogamous relationship today is not the norm. Having multiple partners offers variety. Everybody has something different to offer.

Bedroom Bully '91

I remember when I was like seventeen or eighteen years old living with my grandmother in Brooklyn. She lived on the second floor of a two family house. My older cousin had recently moved out of the first floor. He looked out for me, leaving behind his pull-out couch and keys to the apartment. I already had plans for his pull-out couch, but getting the keys was a bonus. It wasn't long before I started using the crib for chicks to come over, making their face down, ass up. My grandmother never had a clue as to what was going on. So while she was out with relatives at the family bar, I took full advantage of the unmonitored alone time.

There was this one chick who took total advantage of me and the available space. She was tall, at least five feet eight inches, nicely built with a toasted almond complexion and very experienced. I tend to find myself attracted to older women. I especially craved it at that time because she "man handled" my young ass. So I was finally meeting up with Tatiana. Fucking her was going to earn me some brownie points. Anyway, while my grandmother was at the family bar one night, I convinced her to come through. When Tatiana arrived, I brought her upstairs first because I didn't want her to think right off the rip that I was being a dog, even though I was on my "hit it and quit it" routine.

I knew she didn't compare to the average female or what I was used to dealing with. We ended up chilling with my younger uncle for a little while before she suggested we get lost. The moment I had been waiting for. I gave my uncle "the look" to let him know I was headed downstairs with Tatiana. He knew to warn me if his mom (my grandmother) came home before we were finished. I doubted she would be home anytime soon and didn't care because I was about to be digging in some pussy. When we got into the vacant apartment the first thing she asked was, "Is there a bed in here?" On that note, I went to the couch and started flinging cushions to the floor to set up the pull-out bed.

As I was preparing the sofa bed, dressing it with some sheets, I turned to her and asked, "Is this good enough?" To my surprise, when I looked up, she was already letting it all hang out. Shirt and bra were off. It wasn't long before I had a bulge in my pants from the sight of her naked body. She had a hairy kitty-cat, dark nipples, and some juicy, full lips. She walked towards me smiling and reached her hand out towards my pants. It was happening so fast that my pants were undone and down around my ankles within seconds. She definitely took the lead.

At this point, I took my shirt off. She had her hands inside of my boxers, sliding them down slowly. I could feel her soft hands caressing the sides of my hips and thighs. I noticed her stare at my erection. I stepped out of my boxers and Tatiana pushed me on the bed. I quickly realized how thin the mattress was, as springs jabbed in my back. Yet, I wasn't about to complain to fuck up what was about to go down. I took that pain because pleasure was sure to follow. I positioned myself on the bed as she watched with deception in her eyes. I laid on my back figuring she was going to hop right on my dick, when instead she grabbed it and jerked it slowly.

Her hand wrapped around the shaft of my dick with a firm grip. I was stretched out on the bed enjoying the feeling of her kissing and blowing on the head of my dick. When her tongue began to rapidly brush the head of my dick, I could barely keep my eyes open. When Tatiana and I made eye contact I could tell she enjoyed being in control of this situation. That's when she wrapped her mouth around my cock and began to deep throat it. I was mesmerized at how she sucked on it hard and fast, then slowly came up when I could see the spit drip from her mouth onto the head of my cock. She came back down and took me all the way in until her lips met my pubic hairs. I sure wasn't expecting all this extra stuff. This girl was a pro.

I was definitely intimidated by her at this point. She had total control and I felt helpless. She started to slide my dick out of her mouth. It was left wet on my stomach as she made of trail of gentle kisses up my chest until she reached my neck. As she made her way up to my neck, I fondled her roughly. With my hands all over her ass and a couple of fingers invading her wet pussy, Tatiana threw her tongue in my mouth. We were kissing frantically while I had three fingers going in and out of her hot box. Tatiana couldn't take it anymore and snatched my fingers out of her pussy and lowered herself down onto my love muscle.

There was so much moaning and heavy breathing that if somebody came through the front door we would be caught instantly. As she rode me, I began to thrust my dick into her pussy as she came down on me. Tatiana screamed while I moaned. She placed her hands firmly on my chest and sat upright on my dick, putting her in a better position to regain control. Pushing down on my chest, Tatiana slid up and down on my cock with such speed that I called out to her.

"Tatiana, I'm about to cum. Ohhh shit." She replied, "Cum then, come-the-fuck-on-then, I'm cumin' with youuuu." Each word was blurted out in between thrusts. After we climaxed she continued to ride me.

Tatiana was determined to keep riding me until I became flaccid, which wasn't too long after I finished. We had no fan and it was in the middle of the summer, damn there 90 degrees.

It was so hot that day. Now even hotter in the crib, given

what had just transpired. We were both parched and dripping with sweat. I thought it was a job well done. Come to find out, we were just getting started. She insisted we were taking a little break. There was a part of me that wanted to run for safety, yet I chose to endure whatever she had in mind. At first, she wasn't going to let me go to get water because she was ready to start fucking again. I needed a brief escape though. I run upstairs to get us something to drink, as she waited on the bed naked. As soon as I returned and closed the door, she demanded I strip naked because she wasn't done.

She made sure I wouldn't be doing much of anything. She took charge again on round two. I never moaned so much in my life. She had her way with me in almost every position possible on that crappy, make-shift bed. When she left, I was totally exhausted, laid out, face down. To be honest, I never attempted to call her much after that. I would just wait for her to holla at me. She asked or expected a lot from me sexually. I had no intention of this being an everyday thing. The truth is, I was intimidated by her sexual appetite. I didn't need her anyways. I had other chicks lined up. I couldn't deal with how much sex she required. It was hard to keep sneaking her in my grandmother's house. That ended as quickly as it started.

Be All You Can Be
'96-'97

I knew this female named Chastity. She'd always been a good friend of mine. She was tall with a fudge brownie complexion and full figure. I had the pleasure of having sex with her a while back and knew she was not restricted to any individual. One night, we were at my nigga Turk crib with her and this other chick. My other man Biz was there as well. Everybody was drinking, smoking, and just enjoying the mood. Chastity announced she was leaving in two days for boot camp. She had enlisted herself in the army and insisted we celebrate her big departure. She also made it perfectly clear that she wanted to get fucked good before she left.

Turk and I looked at one another in amazement. Did she want more than one of us? Even his shorty was shocked to hear Chastity be so forward. She mainly wanted me, but the other dudes were a bonus for her. Biz was in the living room, so he had no idea what was about to transpire. Turk's shorty started playing him really close, especially when Chastity made it clear that she wanted to be grouped. I got up to let Biz know we had a long night ahead of us. As soon as he heard what she craved, he was all smiles. I think he was a bit skeptical, thinking it may be a prank. So to prove that Chastity was serious, we followed her into Turk's bedroom where she gave a preview of what was to come. When Turk finally came to see what was going on, Chastity was giving Biz head and I was slow fucking her from behind.

Even Turk's shorty came to see what was going on. She only snuck a quick peek and then yanked on Turk to get out the room with her. Every now and then I would thrust my cock into her crotch hard, causing her to bite Biz. I found it funny, but obviously he didn't so she would just take his dick out of her mouth. Then we decided to move this episode into the living room where we had more room to wild-out. Since Chastity was true to her word, we promised to give her something to remember. I went to the living room to make sure it was clean. I popped a porn tape into the VCR and pressed play.

The living room had wall to wall carpeting with a six-piece living room set, a 55-inch fish tank and large entertainment center. The purple light from the fish tank along with the light from the T.V. was more than enough for us to see. So I decided to dim the living room lights before going to grab some condoms.

I had to inform Turk of what was about to go down, being that we were still in his crib. When I returned to the living room, I saw Biz and Chastity enjoying the porno flick and began to strip down to my boxers and socks. Chastity jumped up and began to follow my lead, not stopping until she was completely naked. Biz was the last to strip down. While he was undressing, I told her to finish him off.

She didn't know him well, so I had to make sure she treated him like she would me. Plus, I knew he liked getting head way more than I did. It wasn't something that I was interested in because females always talk about how well they can do it and then disappoint me. I have literally fallen asleep on a couple of bitches while they were giving me head. Damn shame. So he sat on the couch and she got on her knees, stuffing his dick into her mouth. I stood and watched her go to work on my boy while I smoked a clip of weed.

I knelt down behind Chastity, rubbing her fat ass before two fingers found her pussy. With my other hand, I started to masturbate as I rapidly finger fucked her. She shook her ass as I slipped my fingers in and out of her hairy pussy. At the same time, she was sucking the shit out of Biz's dick, making him moan real loud. I was ready to let my pole invaded her kitty but not before I put on a condom. Her pussy juice was all over my fingers when I pulled them out to put on the rubber. When Biz noticed I was about to slide up in her he said, "My dude, don't make her bite me." I just smiled as I grabbed my dick and plunged it into Chastity's soaking wet pussy. I took into account what I caused her to do to Biz, so I didn't go crazy on her. Although, whenever she would pause from sucking him off, I would beat it up. Biz cheered me on, as Chastity was grunting and jerking him off viciously.

We all were considerate enough to make sure nobody felt left out. I would ease up on her so she could continue to give Biz a blow job. We let this go on for a little while longer before switching positions. I decided to sit on the floor instead of the couch and turned her around to face me. It was now my turn to give her a mouth full, as Biz terrorized her pussy. As Biz strapped up, Chastity began to remove the condom off my dick and kiss it repeatedly. With every kiss, she looked up at me with a smile. So I said, "You missed it, huh?" She replied, "Yes I did!" "Well show me how much."

Before I could say another word she had my dick so deep in her mouth. I felt her lips by my balls. Then she slowly brought her juicy lips back up the shaft of my cock until she was kissing the head again. It felt unbelievably great and as I held myself up she forcefully deep throated my penis. Biz stood watching in amazement at how she was rapidly pounding and retracting my dick in her mouth. When she started to lick, suck, and kiss my entire penis, Biz came to his knees to penetrate her. She pulled her mouth away and let out a sigh as she stroked my cock with her hand. I slid back until she was no longer within reach of me. She proved that her head game was on point. My ass sure stayed awake this time.

Once Biz was done beating her pussy up, we kept her on her hands and put one knee on the couch and one on the floor. We both took turns drilling our dicks into her wet pussy. Next, we took turns sitting on the couch and letting her ride us like a cowgirl. She leaned forward, touched the floor, and worked her ass using her hips. She was the one that was leaving, but I felt like she was giving me a gift. We took a brief intermission to get some refreshments and quickly picked up where we had left off. Nobody was done yet. I had smoked that little clip of weed so I was high, but not to the point where I couldn't function. It made everything we were doing feel even better. We laid her down on her back in the middle of the living room. She was holding her legs up in the air and we began to jackhammer her crotch. When she couldn't keep her legs up any longer, we repositioned her.

We had her head at the foot of the sofa. We kept bangin' up the pussy while pinning her legs to the seat of the couch. That night the room was filled with sighs, moans, grunting, and praises. Chastity could handle everything we through at her; titty fucking, and tea bagging included. When all was said and done, we watched as Chastity laid naked on the floor, unable to move or open her eyes. We broke daylight, sitting up in amusement about what just happened.

When Turk walked into the living room the first thing he said was, "I know you nigga's ain't kill her in my crib." Looking at her on the floor, sprawled out and motionless, one would wonder what happened to her. Just as me and Biz laughed at his comment,

Chastity sat up looking in Turk's direction. When she made it to her feet grabbing her panties and headed toward the bathroom she said, "They gave me the best going away gift any bitch could ask for." Then she thanked all of us for being so good to her. We left her there. I went home. I needed sleep, my ass was spent. She was good. Army here she comes, full of protein.

Confession 3

There was this female named Bianca. She made me take a better look at myself, do some self-reflecting. It was a fucked up situation that left me completely confused honestly. She was my girlfriend… a good girl in the hood that I was doing wrong. Her family didn't play that running the street shit, so she was in the house, if not with me. Once we had sex, I was open off of it. Bianca was the sweetest girl I came across in a long time and it was that sweetness that had me head over heels. She went above and beyond to please me. Not only sexually, but mentally. Everybody in my circle approved of her and I think that made it even more special. My family's approval meant the world to me. Bianca was totally accepted by them. So, I made sure she never had to deal with any chicks confronting her, since I was still creeping. One day she let me know she was going to Florida with her family on vacation. I missed her the whole time she was gone, even though I was still doing me. I missed her because I was totally attracted to her in so many ways. When I was with my homies, I had to front like I wasn't pressing her.

I couldn't wait for her to come back and as soon as she returned, my pager bleeped. She asked me to meet her, which I was more than happy to do. When she arrived she wasn't looking happy. In fact, she looked as if she'd been crying. Holding her in my arms, I asked what was wrong. When she looked up at me she said, "Pa, please don't get upset!" Tears ran down her face. I didn't know what to make of it. I assumed the worst, possibly that she'd even slept with another guy. I was 18 years old and how she was acting had me all puzzled. I never experienced the emotional breakdown of a female I was involved with. To be frank, I never saw any female breakdown like that.

The next words out of her mouth were, "When I was in Florida, I had a miscarriage." I was in a state of shock. Her words took me by surprise and I was speechless for a minute. Stunned, I finally stuttered, "You had a miscarriage? I didn't even know you were pregnant!" I am not even sure what her response was, but I know she didn't like my reaction. I mean, I was curious to know how it happened. All she had to say was it must have been from all the rides at Walt Disney. When I said, "Why would you get on rides like that if you knew you were pregnant?" I believe that was the comment that made her snap. She turned and walked away. To this day, I regret not chasing her when she walked off. I tried calling, but she never responded. She lived around the corner from me and I never saw her again. I looked for her a few times, so I could apologize, but we never crossed paths. I never had a chance to say I was sorry.

I think she felt that I should have been more sympathetic to the situation or that I didn't care. In fact, I cared about her a lot. It was just that I didn't know how to react since I never knew she was pregnant in the first place. Still, I couldn't help but wonder that if I had showed a little remorse or some kind of emotional reaction, we might have seen it though. I felt she was being unfair for walking away instead of staying and hearing me out. I always wondered about her. I actually missed her for a while.

That uncomfortable situation led to a new routine. I was going to the Bronx and other places a lot more often. I was still kind of shell shocked by the whole emotional breakdown with Bianca and it was easier to just not be around. I'm sure this is the reason I started to become so easily upset with emotional bullshit from females. I tried to keep a "no feelings" rule in place, which was virtually impossible as I later came to realize.

I felt that since I didn't understand how to react to serious female emotions I didn't need to stick around for any of it. At that moment, being a playa seemed like a good idea, so I was back on the block with the older dudes. I sort of envied them for all the females they had, the partying and the money making. Deep down inside all I wanted was a second chance with Bianca. However, it was apparent that wasn't going to happen. So I focused even harder on being a playa. I was living a double life, emotionally and mentally. I was dealing with all my own mixed emotions (being a playa and one woman man) which left me with no idea how to deal with females on many levels. It just made it that much harder to cope. That being said... simply dismissing a female before dealing with any emotional bullshit made it easier for me.

I had my share of females slide through the block for the older dudes to view. I gained me props. I have to admit that playing females was simple and I had fun doing it. I didn't know it would catch up with me down the line. If you tried to tell me any different back then, I wouldn't have listened. That's because I rarely dealt with the emotional aspect of my relationships. I a female showed signs of feelings or I sensed a breakdown coming, I would cut them off quick. Eventually, it occurred to me that being a playa meant having no respect for a woman's feelings. This was a conflict of interest for me, because I was raised mostly by women and had the utmost respect for them.

Still, I continued to play women as time went on. It was like a bad habit I had formed. I realized it was disrespectful, but I never put my hands on a woman. I guess that was a poor way to justify what I was doing. A lot of men beat females because they want total control of their woman. Often times, they're just taking out other frustrations on the wrong one. I am glad I am not that type of man. That's how I could validate my actions. I went by the motto: "Fuck the world, before the world fucks you." Now that I think about it, and believe me when it say it, I thought about it real hard. It's a stupid motto. The only one who got fucked seemed to be me. It took longer than I thought to realize it though.

Meanwhile, while hangin' in the Bronx, I met this girl named Mercedes. She was a real sweetheart. She was the prettiest girl I came across during my travels to that particular borough. She was soft spoken, extremely polite and everybody seemed to love her. She didn't live too far from my mother's house, so she was over all the time. It was like she practically lived there, which was a gift and a curse cause at the same time. Catching feeling was inevitable.

I thought I was a man of steel. No female could penetrate my heart. When Mercedes and I made love for the first time, I liked how it felt. I had put on this mix-tape with the hottest R&B songs; that baby making, love making shit. If I recall correctly, we had sex until the tape stopped, paused to flip the cassette, and kept going. I was a fool to fight the feelings I had for Mercedes. **I was really into** her. I fought my feelings just so I wouldn't have to deal with the emotional side of things. So when I was presented with an opportunity to leave town to make some bread, I left with no good-bye. **In some twisted way**, this made room for a possible return with some lie or excuse to make up. However, the truth was that if I could've brought her with me, I would've.

Clueless '92

Her name was Bianca. I viewed her as a Latina Goddess. With all the guys to choose from, she only had eyes for me. The older dudes, and even many of the younger one's, gave me mad props for baggin' her. She used to come and check for me every chance she got and we would just chill. I had other females, but none like Bianca, nor did I respect any of them how I respected her. I would give up everything for her. One day I was playing pool in the game room my family owned when Bianca came looking for me. My shot was interrupted by everybody looking out the window snickering or praising me, "Somebody has to check in." She signaled for me to come outside.

Her pretty smile put me in a trance as I walked out to see what she wanted. I gave her a big hug and a kiss, not caring that people were watching. Bianca was accompanied by her hot ass cousin and some dude she was fucking with that week. He was driving and her cousin was riding shotgun. Bianca asked me if I would go someplace with them, but refused to tell me where. All I could get out of her was that it was a surprise and then she hit me with that innocent look. I couldn't say no. Before I left, I ran back inside to inform my boys that I was gonna be gone for a while, then jumped into the car.

As we pulled off, she introduced me to the dude driving. It was obvious that her cousin had him wrapped around her finger. After the brief introduction, I looked at Bianca and before I could say anything we were kissing. She still refused to let me know where we were going, but she made up for it with all the affection I was getting. We jumped on the parkway and hopped off only two exits away from where we had been. When the car finally came to a halt, I couldn't believe where we were at. We had stopped in the parking lot of a motel. When I gave her a curious look, she just grinned. Without saying a word she leaned over to kiss me and then led me out of the car. I wasn't expecting this, but I'm not the one to argue either. I was about to get some pussy.

Following her to a room, I realized we never stopped at the front desk. It became clear to me that this was premeditated and I was suddenly infatuated with Bianca. She knew I was gonna give up the dick. Once we reached our room, she politely and seductively asked me to have sex with her. She then expressed how she felt about me and asked if I felt the way she did. Bianca stood there looking into my eyes, explaining all the reasons why she felt the way she did. In turn, I expressed to her that I felt the same way and wanted her to be my lady. I doubt I would've said anything to fuck up that moment, but I honestly meant everything I said. We became one as I held her tightly and we exchanged a long passionate kiss. Slowly, we made our way to the king sized bed as we softly caressed each another.

We slowly undressed one another, admiring everything that was revealed. Once we were completely naked, I gently laid her in the bed. I crawled on top of her. I looked at her lying there underneath me feeling she was the one for me. Bianca looked me in the eyes and just pulled me towards her so I could enjoy her, and vice versa. I kissed her on the lips, then sucked on her neck by her ears. I nibbled on her lobes and worked my lips towards her firm, plump breasts. I then licked on her nipples while caressing them with my hands. She started breathing heavily. I went as low as her belly button before I worked my way back up to her lips. Once we locked eyes I whispered to her, "Are you ready?" Her response turned me on. "Sí Papi. Dámelo ahora mismo." It wasn't so much what she said, but how she said it that caused her to get the beating I gave her. I grabbed hold of my dick as she parted her legs welcoming me into her love.

I watched as her eyes roll back when I parted her lips with the head of my penis. As I began to penetrate her tunnel, it had this extra warm feeling. Her pussy wrapped tight around my dick, causing me to sigh with every stroke. We made music in that room. She moaned as I thrust. I sighed with every pump. Her pussy was out of this world. Bianca become more vocal once I threw her thick legs onto my shoulders. "Ay Papi, tu sentirse bien dentro de me," she screamed out. I pushed my cock harder in and out of her extremely wet box.

The more she moaned and screamed, the harder I stroked. I even shouted, "Bianca, I love this pussy," and "Mami, te quiero mucho." We rocked the house that afternoon. Her cousin in the next room over said she heard us. We left there with something to remember and happy to have each other.

Ready or Not Part One
'93

I began to make more trips to the Bronx where my mother and siblings lived. There was just too much crazy shit goin' on in the hood. There was drug dealing and guns blasting off. People constantly got robbed. I didn't want to be one of those individuals, so it was best that I hit the next borough. So when I went to the Bronx to chill, I considered it my down time. Plus, it was a different scene. I still made trips back and forth to the block frequently. I love money. Staying in the Bronx had its advantages over staying in Brooklyn. The biggest bonus was that I could have females come and go as I pleased. There was this girl who was a friend of the family and had a thing for me. She was a Latin bombshell. I even can't front. I was feeling her.

I gave Mercedes all my attention when I was with her and she was the only one who kept me from going to the block. I didn't' chill with her all the time like that though, especially if I hit Brooklyn. Well, there was this one day I made plans to have Mercedes all to myself. I arranged for us to chill in my sister's room with no disturbances and had this late '80's and early '90's slow jam tape. I was trying to set the mood for us to get our fuck on, which we both wanted. She just wasn't aware that I was trying to make it happen that particular day.

Once she arrived, I was all happy and excited about the plans I had for her. I watched her move through the house greeting everybody who was there. By the time she got to me I was all smiles as I escorted her to the bedroom. It was for me to see. I was not trying to share her company with anybody. As Mercedes was closing the bedroom door, I pressed play on the stereo. Once the music began streaming, Mercedes smiled and it was obvious what was on both of our minds. It wasn't long before she came and wrapped her arms around me. I stared in her eyes while I wrapped my arms around her and leaned in for a kiss.

The kiss was long and passionate. I was lost in it. I turned her around as we kissed and I laid her gently onto the bed. After what felt like an endless kiss, we laid there looking at one another in the eyes, trying to read each other's thoughts. After 7's "Ready or Not," and other songs like Baby-Face's "Soon as I get Home" played out of the speakers, we kicked our shoes off to better position ourselves on the bed. I can't front... the music had us in a zone. We shared how we felt about one another in between kisses. It wasn't long before I started kissing and sucking on her neck. It wasn't much longer before my hand was underneath her shirt fondling her breasts. Then we ripped off each other's clothes until we were both completely naked.

Good jams played while we kissed. When our eyes finally locked we couldn't help but smile. Before I knew it, I was kissing on her neck, her chest, sucking her breasts and nibbling on her nipples. All along I was rubbing her vagina and fingering her. She panted heavily. Her nipples were dark and hard as my tongue rapidly brushed against them. My dick was hard and it was time for Mercedes to find out how hard it was. I slowly removed my finger from her kitty cat and replaced it with my hard cock. As I began to penetrate her warm, wet pussy, her hands clawed my back.

Once my dick was completely inside of her, I let out a light sigh of relief. She felt so good and I slowly began to stroke my dick in and out of her. With every long, hard stroke, she let out a moan. We moved with the music. Every song had a different tempo. The day was remarkable with that slow jam tape. And to think it all occurred in a house full of people without any disturbances. When it was all over we just laid there holding one another. Looking at her and listening to the music had me thinking about my life; maybe with her in it. We kissed and joked about what everybody in the house was thinking we had going on in here. While walking her home she asked if she could have the tape. I gave it to her right before we parted. Every time she listens to it, she will always think of me and the love I gave her that day.

Confession 4

I was about 20 years old. I was staying with my homeboy Turk in upstate New York at the time. **I can't front**... the females up top were much friendlier than the ones from the city. I didn't have to say a word. Just being from the city was enough for them. So when I met Misty, she was really on it. Come to find out, Turk had put in a good word on my behalf prior to my arrival. Misty happened to be a good friend of Turk's girl. Knowing she would be around one on the regular, that meant I would be seeing her more than the average female.

I can't front, around this time I never thought white chicks came with fat asses. That turned out to be a myth. Misty was short with blue eyes and dirty blonde hair, thick all over. Her ass was big and round; what we call a "black girl ass." I couldn't believe how she was shaped and acted so hood. She played the block, rocked the latest urban wear, and even understood and spoke slang. The funny shit is, she believed since I wasn't from there that she could run game on me. Little did she know, I was so far from getting caught up by any female. She had another thing coming.

Don't get me wrong. I did reap the benefits of her being on my dick, but it also come with headaches. I realized that it wasn't all that attractive when a female tried to be something they are truly not. That hood/gangsta shit is cute, but it damn sure isn't sexy. At that time, I definitely thought it was cute, yet not enough to commit to it. Misty did damn near anything I needed her to do as long as I gave her my time. She was trying too hard to get me to commit, but still doing her own thing like I wasn't aware. So when I started to get around and hang with other females, it was then I realized how much Misty was on me. Often times, people show they care or like you when you begin to show interest in someone else. Then they act out to be noticed or seek attention.

Misty was trying to buy my love by assisting me in gettin' money. She believed as long as she handled shit for me that I would commit to her. It became obvious that all I had to do is fuck her at least three times a week and she was at my beckoning call. It was her who made me realize that I could get certain females to do whatever I wanted just for a fuck. On top of that, being around Misty's circle of friends had also brought to my attention to the fact that they were willing and ready to give it up too. It wasn't just a white girl thing either because all of her friends were either black or bi-racial, except for one or two. I could really have my cake and eat it too.

Around the same time, I met another female known for gettin' money. Her name was Venetia. She was well known in town due to her previous man. That being said, it meant that I wouldn't allow her to get too close to me in the business sense. Yet as I got to know her, she wasn't that bad of a person. I did notice that she thought we would become a hot money getting couple and take the hood by storm. I was upfront about my intentions but these women believed they had what it took to change all that. Ironically, I notice that there are many females who pre-fer to settle with someone who lies and cheats on them. That's only if he's popular, attractive, or making good money. To most, this was considered to be what a good man was and being open and honest made a good man no good. Many men have treated women so disrespectfully that it seems to be the norm for some. I think that a lot of women who know what they want out of a man know when he is of good caliber and substance. Women who deal with men that live that street life only know of the lies, cheating, and the disrespect because these men don't know how to treat a decent woman. They end up turning a decent woman bad over time. When they decide that they no longer want any part of a street nigga and want a man that says thank you, opens doors, and pulls out chairs; they can't get one because they are damaged. At that point they typically have kids and are searching for someone to play house with. They seek a man with his shit together but don't allow the time for things in a new relationship to be established. They demand that a man should play a certain role from day one and it doesn't usually work like that.

Women who find themselves out in the streets and want Prince Charming end up mad when they don't get it after awhile. How? Why? What man is going to want a women that sells drugs and most likely has two or three kids and hang out all types of late hours of the night? Don't have your own apartment, no car, didn't finish school, and most likely the group of niggas you running with has seen the inside walls of your pussy a couple of times… but you want respect? NO! These upstate girls let anything go. They accept too much.

This Boy is Mine
'93-'94

During my traveling years, I crossed paths with a lot of women who had little to no respect for one another. Even if it had been made clear that a female was involved with a certain man, there always seemed to be another female that would pursue the same man anyways. My first experience of this kind of behavior was with two females that I met who knew one another prior to meeting me. The first female named Misty was stuck on me as soon as we were introduced. She did everything she could to get my attention... which wasn't too hard to do. Her body was outrageous for a white girl. That's all it took for me. It wasn't long before she was throwing the pussy at me like rice at a wedding.

One night my man decided to stay out with his girl for the night, leaving Misty and I home alone. I found it cute that Misty made it clear we were fucking. I made it very clear that we were fucking alright but in my man's bed and not on the cheap air mattress on the floor. That took her by surprise because that's one thing she never thought of doing. Unlike Misty, I was not scared of Turk or his shorty. It took some time but I finally convinced her to agree to my terms and we made our way to Turk's bedroom. She still seemed a bit hesitant though.

I began to strip down while saying, "Misty—the reward is worth the risk." Within seconds I was standing in front of her butt ass naked with the moonlight shedding light on my body. It was then that she said, "Fuck it—I won't tell." I watched as she undressed, lusting over her fat ass as she pulled her pants and underwear down. I still thought it was crazy for a white girl to have such a big booty. Misty blushed as I admired her naked body and pulled her onto the bed. As soon as she got comfortably positioned on her back, I began to fondle her. It was a tiny room and Turk had a full size bed with very little room for anything except for a dresser with a T.V. on it. The blinds were open causing the room to be well lit by the street lights.

I looked her over. I noticed how pink her nipples were and the blonde hair that covered her vagina. She just laid there eyeing my erection. My fingers parted her fat pussy lips. As I slowly started to slide my three fingers into her vagina she sighed. My thumb played with her clit as I pushed my fingers inside of her. I watched her wiggle about with her eyes closed. She reached out for my fully erect penis saying, "I want you inside of me." I pulled my fingers out of her wet pussy about to go for a condom when she sat up and grabbed hold of my dick.

She jerked me off with a firm grip. Misty stroked my dick like a crazed woman before pulling me towards her as she lied back down. I followed her lead, nibbling on her nipples. I only stopped to reach for the condom. She watched impatiently as I slid it on. Instead of climbing back on top, I told her to let me hit it from the back. She smiled as she slowly got on her hands and knees. She knew she had a valuable asset and how much it was worth.

I positioned myself behind her with one knee on the bed and my other foot planted on the floor. I watched as she reached between her legs and grabbed my dick and placed it at the entrance of her juice box. As soon as the tip of my dick parted her lips I pushed forward to penetrate. After a few strokes, Misty did something I never experienced before. She contracted her pussy muscles, causing it to squeeze extra tight around my dick. It was a new, good feeling. I pounded my rocket in and out of her. She expressed how great the dick was for her and she didn't want it to stop, as my thighs smacked up against her butt cheeks. I was watching as my dick rapidly entered and exited her juicy vagina.

I decided I wanted her on her back so I suddenly, without warning, pulled out. She turned back with a disappointed look on her face. She thought I was just going to leave her hanging but that wasn't the case. Not at all. I told her to turn over so I could finish enjoying her good pussy. She did so with pleasure. Her nipples were hard. I couldn't resist the urge to suck and nibble on them. I lifted both of her legs, placing them on my shoulders as she reached between her legs to guide my penis into her. I leaned forward once inside of her, pushing her feet damn near behind her head. **It wasn't too long before I reached my climax and released her legs so I could relax.** After that night, she committed herself to satisfying me whenever possible. The best thing was that she was fully aware it was all on my terms; which still didn't stop her from trying to win my heart so I would make her my lady.

Over the next few days I was introduced to a lot of Turk's associates and friends. His roommate showed me around town a bit more. It was because of him that I came in contact with Venetia. She was a black chick with a fat ass. She was as thick as Misty, just a little taller. She knew Misty. Venetia had Turk's roommate tell me to get at her when I ditched Misty.

Turk let me know that she was feeling me and wanted to break me off. There were a couple of cheap shots made at me because Misty was white. I finally got up with Venetia and put her in her place. First and foremost, I let her know I'm only down for a booty call. She responded, "Do you fuck with white girls because you're scared of black chicks?" In turn I said, "I'm only scared of one thing and it doesn't start with a color or end with chicks." She must have thought that she was gonna rock my world to the point I wouldn't fuck with another white girl. Once she laughed, I knew I had her regardless of who I was fucking.

We then made plans to hook up and get our fuck on, and she made it clear I better not let her down. I think she was just jealous that Misty was getting more of my time than she was. Misty was not thrilled with Venetia's sudden and frequent visits. Nor was she blind to the fact that Venetia was definitely throwing herself at me. As I learned more about Venetia, it was evident that she felt like she was better than Misty. It was as if she had more to offer or she was going to put it on a nigga good enough so that she could get all the attention to outshine Misty. I really didn't care what back and forth shit they needed to hash out among themselves. I was going to be fucking them both.

It became a big contest to see who had the most to offer until they realized I was gonna "do me" regardless. With that being known but not completely understood, Venetia and I pre-pared for the showdown. I had her come over one evening when Misty wasn't around so we could chill. She had a lot of slick shit to say. She thought that she was better than other chicks that I came to know around this city. I didn't see what was so great that she was trying to offer. She was hustling like I was and had kids. Right there, her priorities were not straight. That is not someone I could see myself with on a regular basis. I told her to relax. I wasn't with all the slick talking and shut her up with a kiss. Mind you this time my man, his girl, and his roommate were home so we were in the living room. The whole apartment was too small for all these people to be staying there.

I wasn't sure if somebody would walk in on us. I blew up the cheap air mattress and dressed it up before laying on it. That night I performed terrible and realized that the sneaky, quiet shit was not working for me. That didn't stop Venetia from telling Turk's roommate that I couldn't keep up. So I sent word to her that I needed to holla and to get at me. When we finally got up with each other I told her I had found a crib and wanted her to break it in. Venetia had agreed to bless the crib and told me not to disappoint her. I had just gotten the keys to my large, one bedroom apartment with wall to wall carpet. I took some blankets from Turk's house and borrowed his vacuum. When she arrived at my crib she already knew what it was, so our clothes came right off. Venetia's body was nicely shaped with a Hershey chocolate complexion. The hair surrounding her vagina was extremely thick, just like her thighs.

She stood about 5 feet 6 inches tall, medium to dark skin complexion, with nice breasts and very dark nipples. I led her to the living room where we were going to bless it with vigorous sex. The blankets were spread out on the carpet to avoid rug burns and being that we were on the third floor I didn't bother to hang up any blinds. As we made our way to the blankets on the floor, I realized she was staring at my erection. A real unexpected look appeared on her face when she finally looked up at me, because she knew this was going to be good. Once I got her comfortably on her back, I parted her legs. Right then she reached between her legs and parted her pussy lips revealing her clit. I quickly began rubbing it with my thumb as I put two fingers in her pussy to finger fuck her. I wanted her wet and ready for what I was about to do to her. I wanted her to leave there knowing she'd be calling back for more.

Venetia was quickly up on her elbows watching as I played with her pussy while slowly stroking my dick. She then looked up at me and said in a seductive voice, "Fuck me. Fuck me right now." Before she could say another word, her legs were in the air as I slid my cock into her jungle of love. Once inside of her, I started to thrust my dick repeatedly into her rain forest. She was moaning uncontrollably and I went King Kong on the pussy, swinging my dick on that shit like I was Tarzan. We were making so much noise that it echoed throughout the empty apartment and maybe the whole building. We fucked like two wild animals in every position possible until we both reached our climax.

We were both very satisfied. I told her how much I couldn't wait to get some furniture. She agreed with me. The next time I saw Turk's roommate, he gave me props for smashing Venetia.

Great Adventures
'93 & '01

I've had my share of booty calls, but there was only one female that I met who truly knew the meaning. Her name was Nishka. The only thing we did was fuck. No long conversations or anything of that nature. We never took any interest in one another's hobbies, goals, or financial status. The only thing we were concerned about was each other's sexual needs. Nishka was an opportunist in the sense that any chance she got to have sex with me, she seized it. What was even more beautiful about the relationship we had is that all of our sexual encounters happened outside of the home.

Nishka was on the shorter side with a dark chocolate complexion. She was thick in the right places. She had a sexy aura about her. Her hair came down to her shoulders. She had a full set of lips and her cheekbones were high. She was shaped like a Coca-Cola bottle, the glass ones, with a fat ass. Now that I think about it, Nishka was a beautiful black female as far as her looks were concerned. She was about those Benjamin's and did what she had to do to get them. To be truthful, I don't have the slightest idea what made her take to me the way she did. I mean she did whatever I asked of her whether it was sexually or not. At the end of the day, I just settled for a quick fuck here and there though.

Once in a while, I would involve a friend to partake in an adventure with Nishka. I respected our relationship and how she handled herself as a female; one who knew what she wanted, when she wanted it, how to get it and where to get it from. At the same time, she kept it all concealed to those on the outside looking in. To top it off, I wasn't one to pass judgment or criticize her about her ways. Maybe that was the reason why Nishka dealt with me the way she did with no question or objections. Whatever the reasons, I was honored that I received the benefits without the hard work. I could only imagine what some guys had to go through.

The first time we fucked was after leaving the club one night. I was with my cousin, Nishka, and her sister-in-law. They were all liquored up and high from smoking so much weed. Nishka and I were passed that stage though. So when Nishka told me to follow them as we headed out, I knew I was about to fuck. As for my cousin, I really wasn't too concerned about him getting laid just as long as he followed them. That was due to the fact that neither one of us, Nishka or me, were driving at the time.

We followed them up to the projects that shorty lived in, which was in a secluded area. It looked deserted because it was so dark going up that spiral road. We pulled in the parking lot of her building and found a spot. My cousin and I got out and walked over to the car they were in. It was real late so everything was quiet and dark as hell. Once Nishka stepped out of the car my cousin got into the car to holla at shorty. Me on the other hand took Nishka by the hand and led her to the back of the car. There was nothing to talk about and I threw her against the trunk as I looked around to make sure nobody was looking. Once I finished checking out my surroundings, I pressed up against her and started fondling her. I was sucking on her neck and ear while sliding my hand up her short skirt. Taking my fingers and working past her panties I began playing with her pussy.

Once my fingers were inside of her, she held me tight as she panted. I guess we were rocking the car because I heard her sister-in-law say, "Calm down you two." Removing my hand from between her legs I took her over to the side of the building. As soon as we were out of their sight I pulled out a condom and dropped my pants. At the same time telling her, "Pull up your skirt and drop your panties." Which she did, no questions asked. She turned around to grab hold of the railing.

It was a nice summer evening to be outdoors. I don't think we were out of sight of passing cars. Yet that night we didn't care who saw. In fact, the idea that we could get caught made it that much more exciting. Especially since the only vehicle that could possibly be passing through at that time would be the police. Still, the risk was well worth the reward. As I finished rolling on **the condom**, Nishka looked back at me, still gripping the rail and said, "Fuck me hard Daddy. Hard and fast." I immediately penetrated her black hole.

As she yelled out commands, I rammed my pipe into her repeatedly, making her to moan. "Oohh Yes! Yes baby! Give it to me just like that, Daddy!" Leaving one hand on the rail, she used the other to stuff her shirt in her mouth to muffle the moans. I was all up in the pussy, deep stroking it doggy style. I had to admit the pussy was good. She had a nigga toes curling up in his sneakers. Once I saw that it was feeling good to her, I put that work in and wore that ass out until she shuddered and her knees were weak. I am glad she was holding on to that railing for support. I put one of my feet up on the bottom bars on the railing for more leverage and started pounding the shit out of her until I exploded. It was absolutely one of the best nights I had and I was shocked at how easy it was to get her to have sex outside. We seemed to have this unspoken agreement that allowed me to have my way with her. The other crazy thing was it always was an on sight connection, no prearrangement, no questions asked.

I suddenly became this sexual deviant when in her presence. Whenever we interacted it was like there was nobody else to be concerned with. The next time I bumped into Nishka was at the same club but she was by herself. I had one of my homies with me when she approached. I was in a blind spot of the club which also happened to be next to the bar. The bar was located in the back of the club. From where we stood we went unnoticed, or so I thought.

That was the advantage of being where we were, nobody could sneak up on us. She had on a tight top and a short tight skirt with her hair done up. The whole time she was headed towards us I never thought to mention to my boy that I knew Nishka. So when she stopped in front of me with this look that was intended to entice me. He was completely taken back. He was fucking her at one point, not sure what happened to them, but as long as we were good I don't care what they were going through. He must have thought I couldn't pull her, but he also didn't know I was fucking her regularly, until now... Then she turned around and backed her ass up on me, leaning up against my chest and started dancing. Her one hand grabbed hold of my lower thigh, as she placed her other hand on the back of my neck. I looked over at him like I didn't even know her and his jaw dropped to the floor. That's when I whispered in her ear that he was a friend of mine. Nishka removed her hand from my neck, reached over to my friend and shook his hand. She then leaned forward and started shaking her ass on me harder after feeling my erection.

I then decided that I would seize the opportunity to fuck her where we stood. I reached in my pocket to pull out a condom and caught my boy's attention. I motioned for him to stand in front of her for more blockage. Once he was in place, I slide my hand down her thigh and then up her skirt. When she looked back I flashed the condom at her and it was like she read my mind. As I was unzipping my pants she leaned forward placing her hands on my boy's shoulders. As I looked around to make sure nobody was watching. I pulled out my dick and put the condom on. Noticing that nobody was paying us any mind, I slid my dick past her thong and into her tight pussy.

Soon as I was inside of her she begun to push back into me meeting me as I pushed forward. While I was in her honey pot I started to knead her ass cheeks like bread dough. Luckily I had my back against the wall because she was now doing all the work. The only dude who caught on didn't say anything as he stared in amazement. It didn't take too long for me to bust my load. I then signaled to her to let my man get what I just had. Once she smiled I walked up to my dude handing him a condom and gestured to him to go for it. He couldn't believe what I was suggesting yet he didn't hesitate to try. I stood where he was standing and once I felt her hands rest on my shoulders I knew he succeeded.

Nishka never let me down and that shocked me sometimes. There was no limit to what she would do sexually. I can't say I tried everything, yet I doubt she would have refused. I truly had no reason or need to abuse the relationship that we had. The next time we bumped heads was early 2001 at the store me and my people owned. Quite a bit of time had passed. She was doing well for herself. We both couldn't believe our eyes when we saw one another. At this point, I wasn't too sure if what we had was still there between us. So I decided to have her come through later on that night to see if it was still the same.

When she came that night, the store was packed with my niggas. It was after business hours so the studio part in the back was open, but the store front was closed. I introduced her to my dudes. One of my boys had to turn himself in to do some time, so I decided to offer Nishka to him. Before I could try all that though, I had to make sure she was still down for whatever. I took her into the bathroom to see if I could fuck her. It took some persuasion, but I got her to drop her panties and sit on my dick. I let her ride me for a few minutes being that it was a small uncomfortable bathroom. We both were kind of disappointed that we weren't someplace more open. I suggested that she pleasure my boy because he was about to do a bid. After she agreed to give him some head, I stepped out of the bathroom leaving her behind. I walked up to my boy and let him know that my going away present was waiting in the bathroom. He thought at first that I was kidding until I let him know I don't play those games. On that note he disappeared into the restroom while I accepted all the praise for making it go down.

I definitely was feeling like a pimp and probably could have pimped her but that just wasn't my thing. If it had been, than Nishka would've been my bottom bitch because she never let me down.

Confession 5

A t this point and time I was beginning to believe that it didn't pay to be nice to all females. Regardless of how nice or respectful I was to some females they were taking that shit for granted. I came across many females who had been disrespected by dudes mentally and physically for a long time. So for them when I showed affection, love, care, and concern they didn't know how to receive it. They weren't used to a gentleman, someone who was respectful and kind-hearted. It was amazing to see how some females would embrace the abuse and disrespect. They were so used to it they would totally reject a brother who refrained from verbal and physical torture. Some of them felt that, "if it's not rough, it's not right." It amazed me that a woman could think if you don't fight with them or show some kind of jealousy you didn't care. I don't and will never get down like that.

What was inconceivable is that I've met quite a few females who considered a gentleman to be a sucker. This kind of female views a sincere, kind man as a lesser man. It is unfortunate that a lot of men don't know how to treat a female so they figure abuse is the way to go because they don't know anything else. In turn, this causes a female to believe that she can take advantage of a good man. I've attracted a lot of women who thought this to be true. It got to the point that I would try to show them otherwise but it usually proved to be fruitless. It wasn't that I couldn't be what they desired, but they weren't willing to drop an old routine to try something new. Don't get me wrong though. There were times I was pushed and my hand was forced. Those rare occasions ended with me cutting all ties. Over time, I learned to see it coming before it occurred. In turn, this prevented it from happening again.

There was this one female named Skylar who had no clue how to appreciate a good man. She had no desire to earn respect. Instead, she attempted to buy respect with money and sex. This caused a huge misunderstanding between us because I was a gentleman and she believed she had purchased my respect. What she failed to realize was that mind frame wasn't going to get her anywhere. I tried to encourage her to correct her way of thinking. Time and time again I tried because there was something about her that made me postpone turning my back on her. I even proposed that I would fuck with her more exclusively if she would take heed to what I was attempting to show her. Another fruitless attempt and with that I accepted she was stuck in her ways. Sometimes I wonder if I cursed at her and threatened to beat her up like she was used to from others, she probably would have acted right. I won't do those things in order to be with a woman. Too many out here too stoop to that level.

Skylar wanted what she wanted on her time, but never took the proper steps to achieve it. **To this very day**, every time I see her, she acts like I'm the one who played her. I truly believe that she had no clue what a relationship should consist of. I now understand why though. All she knew was a slouch nigga to come in her house, eat all her food, sleep all day, fuck her and have no desire to do anything more with himself. I've come across many women that cater to this type of man, believing it's acceptable. It makes them feel needed. I explained to Skylar that I would've settled down with her, but she didn't know how to appreciate a good brother. One needs to understand that sex, money, and drugs don't equate to respect, loyalty, and happiness. I finally came to the conclusion that some people are stuck in their ways and refuse to change or are simply too afraid of it. To be honest, I wouldn't have settled down with her anyway yet I figured I see how she would respond to the proposal.

I feel bad for Skylar because I believe she deserved a lot more than she chose to settle for. She had the potential to be an outstanding woman instead of a grown-up big girl. She wasn't the only female like that, but she was the only one I put a great amount of effort into despite all the letdowns. I guess I had a soft spot for her and hoped I could help her be the woman I knew she could be. Still, I chose to be good to her and accept that she'd never be able to understand me.

On the other hand, this female named Gisselle actually appreciated my kind demeanor. She wasn't innocent, but she definitely wasn't some hood chick. She came across as this well-educated career woman when I first met her. As I got to know her better, I realized she had one major character defect… she was damaged both mentally and emotionally. On top of that, she extra ditsy. She kept a nice apartment, but attracted the wrong company. She was very polite, soft spoken and loved to cook. Gisselle admitted she had been in numerous abusive relationships. Now, some of my boys were probably in the same category. It's bad when your own homie is on some "smack a chick around" shit. That always made me more determined not to be like them. I didn't want to treat Giselle the same way. I decided to help her out for letting me stay in her house while I was on the run.

All my people told me I didn't owe her anything. This made it evident that most viewed her as just a submissive "yes woman" type. Therefore I questioned her judgment. I didn't try hard to understand why she let people talk to her or treat her with such disrespect. All I could do was give her a taste of respect and loyalty. Treat her as an honorable woman. It was then up to her to expect it at all times. I thought this would help her build some self-respect.

In my eyes, females deserve nothing but respect. However, nowadays fellas give all the respect to the loud, rude and ratchet females. Just good pussy or a nice head game alone doesn't warrant respect. I can't seem to understand how some people want respect when they don't even respect themselves. Once someone has been subjected to abuse repeatedly for years, they begin to fear change. After being in hell for so long, some believe heaven is nothing but wishful thinking. It believe it is my duty to be a gentleman to assist in changing this outlook on life. On the other hand I can't condemn them for being satisfied with how their lives currently are. I just can't help but get discouraged when I see a good thing go to waste, myself included.

It actually hurts me when I have to act other than myself to people. Occasionally, I've had to speak to a female more aggressively or get belligerent so they could comprehend my point. Even if I care about a person, I refuse to entertain certain behaviors or attitudes. I'll still acknowledge the individual, display respect, and might even bust that ass if I run into you in the future. As far as anything else goes, I'd rather pass because I refuse to accept anyone as an equal that has no morals and values. I was feelin' myself at the time. I was the man. So for the dummies reading this, that all means if you didn't act right and behave when I come through, you were getting cut off from the dick. Even now, I never expect everybody to be on the same page, but I do expect them to be reading a similar chapter or be in the same text.

Early Morning Wake Up
'98–'99

I was on the run from a case I had pending. My people let me lay low in a crib they had access to. The shorty the crib belonged to was named Gisselle. She was around 5 feet 10 inches tall and biracial. Gisselle had a swiss almond complexion, a nice bubble butt, large breasts, and a set of full lips. All in all, Gisselle was an attractive young lady. She wasn't loud, rowdy, nor was she known for hanging on the block. Giselle was a soft spoken person and extremely polite to everybody. ·

Still, that meant nothing when it came to how people treated her. Regardless, I didn't let that dictate how I would treat her. Especially since I was staying with her for the time being. We barely saw one another since I was out paper chasing and she was stripping in some gentleman's club. Most of the time we would bump heads early mornings and late evenings or when we decided to give the streets a break. We also agreed that there would be no sexual acts with other people at the crib. If we had any plan to fulfill that need it would take place elsewhere.

Her apartment was a tiny one bedroom that was cluttered with furniture. Still, it had this cozy feeling that helped me to relax. There were plenty of days I didn't even leave the crib, especially on week nights. Even though she didn't have cable, she did have lots of movies and music. I appreciated that. Some people's house only got nine choices and that shit be getting boring as hell. At least I stayed entertained. On the nights when we both home, she took the initiative to cook. I could see that she enjoyed the company and I would have to admit I enjoyed her company as well. As I got to know her it was clear to me that Gisselle was good peoples except for her low self-esteem. That, coupled with her low self-respect, I chose to be a friend instead of pursuing anything more. I thought about it but I felt like I would be taking advantage of her like everybody else.

There was this one particular night that we ended up in the crib together chillin'. We smoked some weed and had a few laughs at her expense. She truly was what you call an airhead and it's sad to say but no wonder she stripped. No disrespect to the strippers, but she was one that had nothing else to offer. Our conversations revolved around movies, music, parties, and bullshit. Still, Gisselle had a good heart and that counts for a lot in my eyes. It wasn't too often we chilled like that prior to that night. We actually had a good time and I for one was glad I did not go out. As the evening came to an end, Gisselle got up from the sofa and straightened up before calling it a night. I helped out and prepared the couch with the blanket so I could do the same.

I finally laid down on the couch and watched Gisselle walk towards her room. She was wearing a silk two piece pajama set and I noticed how plump her ass was without jeans on. I looked at her with a new lust in my eyes as I realized how nice her ass was as. Nevertheless, I rolled onto my side facing the back of the couch and closed my eyes to go to sleep. All of a sudden I heard her voice say, "I know the couch isn't that comfortable. You are welcome to come sleep in the room with me." She followed that up by saying, "But you have to keep your hands to yourself." I responded back by saying, "Please Gisselle, don't flatter yourself." I took her up on her offer though. I do admit that it was hard to get real comfortable without being all on her. Gisselle's full size bed definitely wasn't big enough to share with someone she didn't want touching her. I genuinely had no intention of actually trying anything because she had made that slick remark though. We both rolled over in opposite directions and fell out. I actually had a peaceful night sleep.

I am not too sure what time it was when I woke up. All I know is that it was light outside. When I looked over, Gisselle was laying there asleep with her back to me. I had slept on my stomach and turned on to my side facing Gisselle. I let my hands say "Good Morning" and started rubbin' up on her. She poked her booty back at me and my dick got hard. I leaned up on my elbow and my other hand touch and show great tenderness on her waist, thighs, hips, and ass.

It wasn't until I started to massage her ass cheeks that she rolled over onto her stomach. I smiled because she didn't turn her head to face me or even move away. Instead, she gave me access to her whole backside as she played possum. I got aroused by this game she was playing, pretending to be asleep. I played along 'cause I was curious to see how it would end. I started to massage her lower back but now my hand found its way under her pajama top. Her skin was warm and soft, I then slid my hand into her pajama bottom. Once my hand came in contact with her soft butt, Gisselle's legs parted. After sliding my hands into her panties and caressing her bare ass, my dick began to throb. I couldn't wait much longer to begin sexually assaulting her. Still I couldn't help but find it cute that Gisselle still pretended like she was asleep.

Spreading her legs made me realize that Gisselle didn't want me to stop. That's when I slid my hand past the crack of her butt until I reached her vagina. I was amazed at how fat her pussy was and at how wet she already was. Gisselle arched her back as I slid my fingers into her. I played with it for a few minutes, as she was still fake sleeping. I removed my hand from inside her as I pulled back the sheets. I took my boxers off to put on a condom.

I then slowly began to pull down Gisselle's pajama bottoms and panties. The whole time I was undressing her, she never said a word or even looked at me. I kneeled on the bed to get in position on top of her. I had her legs between mine. I parted her legs a little

63

wider. Being an observant type of person, I noticed her huge clit poking out from its hiding place. It was like a tiny punching bag, waiting for me to beat it up.

I was fascinated by the size of her clit. Had she been my shorty, I would have sucked on it like a pacifier. Instead, I used the tip of my dick to beat it up as she pushed her ass in the air. She squirmed around a whole lot. I could hear her panting. To my surprise, Giselle decided that she was going to be a part of the fun and officially "wake up." She turned over and told me to put my dick in her face. I did as I was told and was almost sitting on her chest. Gisselle took my dick and put it in her mouth and sucked on it like it was a popsicle. That shit felt so good I didn't know if I was going to drop from the sensation of her warm mouth or the electrifying jolt I got from the tight squeezing around my dick.

Giselle began to stroke and suck my dick all at the same time. Her other hand rolled my balls around. I had never felt such pleasure all at once. That's when she did the ultimate. She circled her finger around my asshole. My dick stiffened up. I had no idea my shit could ever get that hard. I had never felt anything like it. I was mad and felt awkward that she was even doing it, but at the same time that shit felt like I could have exploded right then. I had to hold it together because I didn't want to cum yet. I needed to fuck her but she was doing all this shit at the same time, I wasn't sure if I could hold on any longer.

Gisselle licked my dick like it was melting ice cream. She lifted my dick and licked it from the bottom, up. She did this flickering thing with her tongue around my ass. This was a fight I surely wasn't winning. I had to hold on to the wall and try to keep my head up. It was difficult. I started talking in tongues that shit felt so good. I don't know what I was saying. She had skills and I definitely was keeping her on speed dial. I had to pull my dick out of her mouth. I couldn't take anymore. I told her to turn over and get on her hands and knees. She was about to get it.

Grabbing hold of her ass cheeks, I slid completely inside of her and then retracted. I continued like that nice and slow enjoying all of her wetness. My dick was so coated with her dampness. It was exhilarating to see my dick enter and exit her juicy vagina at a slow pace. Her fat pussy lips wrapped around the shaft of my dick with a firm grip. She was now moaning uncontrollably into the pillow, which muffled the noise as I began to speed up. Soon I was viciously and rapidly pounding my dick into her pussy. I let go of her ass cheeks and leaned on top of her as I continued beat up the kitty. I slid out of her sticky sweet love hole and dipped back into it nice & slow. I whispered into her ear, "Good Morning. Is that how you like it?" She lifted her head up from the pillow and screamed out, "Yes, yes, yes, yes!!"

I continued to taunt her until I busted a nut. I let out a loud sigh of relief. After I pulled out of her I rolled over onto my back. She looked opposite my direction and said, "Thank you." Afterward we continued to have early morning sex whenever I slept over Gisselle's crib.

False Hope '04–'05

Skylar was her name. We had been messing around for a long ass time, off and on with no real commitment. We went through brief periods of entertaining one another. She had it bad for me but her habits caused me to keep it simple on a surface level. We had an understanding though. If I was coming through everything was getting shut down. Whoever was there had to go and all other plans ceased.

Skylar had a French vanilla complexion with pretty green eyes. Skylar was half black, half white with a nice set of tetas and a big ass. Even though she was stubborn, I tolerated her.

One day, I decided to pop in on her unannounced to see what she was up to. As soon as she opened the door and seen me, a smile came across her face. I was invited into her home which was put together real nice. Skylar always seemed to be thrilled whenever I stopped by or bumped into her in the streets. As soon as I sat down at the kitchen table I noticed that she had a bottle of cognac and ditches on deck. Besides drinking and smoking, Skylar loved to cook. So when I announced that I was planning on chilling if she wasn't doing anything, she quickly welcomed me.

Her apartment was small for a duplex. Probably because it belonged to housing. All the bedrooms were upstairs, along with the bathroom. The living room and dining area was off the kitchen. So once I stepped in her house I was in the dining room looking into the living room by the kitchen. Skylar had it furnished nicely and also had two kids that I was fond of. They knew me well enough to know I don't cater to their wants and sassy behaviors. Skylar knew what I liked and always tried to use it to keep me around but I knew it wasn't truly how she was.

So while sitting at the table kicking it with one another, I reminded her that I was hungry. As we sat chit chatting, I brought some things to conversation. I didn't approve of some of her ways. Skylar agreed to slow down for the night while I was around. She should've realized I planned on staying there as soon as she saw me take out my bottle and place it next to hers.

Skylar made macaroni and cheese with some barbeque beef ribs for dinner. Every now and then the kids would make their presence known and then disappear quickly. We had already taken multiple shots. I had more than her. By the time the food was cooked, I was feelin' nice and ready to chow down.

We watched a movie to spend some one on one time with the kids before smoking another blunt and drinking too much. I watched Skylar as she picked up after the kids in her sweatpants and sports bra. The outfit revealed how nice her ass and breasts were. I felt the need to share that with her so she knew I had my eyes on her. I vaguely recall her saying something like, "This all could be yours if you would do what you're supposed to." All I could do was smile. I knew her only real complaint was that she hadn't chilled with me in awhile.

As time passed and the evening fell upon us, we were both ready for some real alone time. Her daughter was occupied watching television. However, her son was reluctant to stay in his room. She spoiled the shit out of him regularly. This one day though, she was mad at herself for it. He was the baby and wouldn't fall asleep until she rocked him. That frustrated her. I joked around and told her I was going to go home if he kept up.

"Sit your ass down and stop worrying about him," I told her. She moved to stand in front of the door, blocking my way. I went on to say, "I ain't really going no where." With a look of disbelief she said, "I don't care if you do. Leave you fucking liar."

Skylar started to rant. "I can't stand your black ass." I just laughed and replied, "You know you love my black ass so just shut up. Now put mama's boy to sleep so I can get some of Mama's you know what." She put her attention back on her boy while I prepared myself another drink. Eventually he cried himself to sleep. Skylar was concerned it might be an ear infection. She sat with a huge sigh of relief as she lit the blunt I left in the ashtray.

Skylar got up to sit on my lap at the table, where I was sipping my Hennessey. I mentioned that he would most likely wake up again shortly. Her response was that she better had got some dick before he does and slowly began to rock on my lap. With that being said, there was nothing else for us to talk about. I told her that I wanted to have sex right where we were sitting at. She leaned back, still working her lower half and said, "You don't want to move because you're fucked up, huh?" I looked at her and said, "Do you want some dick or not?" Before she could respond I reached around and grabbed her breasts. I gripped them firmly, as Skylar leaned back against me so I could suck on her neck. The only light came from the glow of the television.

Finally, I slipped my hand underneath her sports bra, making it lift to reveal her perky tatas. I nibbled on her earlobes while massaging her breast. My dick was rock hard. I had about enough of this foreplay. I took one hand and slid it down into her pants, quickly finding her pussy. Skylar breathed heavily as I slipped two fingers inside of her. She continued gyrating her hips. It wasn't long before she stood up and pulled her pants down to her ankles. She took only one foot out of her pants then spun around to unbuckle my belt. Once she got my belt unbuckled, I pulled off my other garments and threw on a condom.

I sat down. Skylar leaned over, preparing to sit on my hardness.

She placed her hands on my knees then lowered herself onto me as I guided my rock hard cock into her pussy. At that moment I knew why I couldn't leave her alone. Her pussy was slippery and wet, always ready for me. She rode my dick good. I stared at the ceiling, breathing heavily as her ass smacked against my thighs. I lifted my head back up when she began to slow down. I wondered what she was doing. To my surprise, she was bending over to touch the floor as she backed that ass up. I grabbed hold of her waist thinking she might fall. Skylar whispered, "Move. I got this." So I did as she asked. With that, she popped her ass up and down on me rapidly.

I sat back and enjoyed the sight of her pussy gliding back and forth on my dick. I caught myself making all kinds of stupid faces. Suddenly, in a demanding tone she asked, "Do you love this pussy?" "Yes," I responded with no hesitation. She then said, "Do you love how it feels on your dick?" "Yes I do. It feels great. Don't stop." She started to speed up at that point. As she moaned and thrusted she got the words out, "How about that? Do you like it like that?" So of course I shouted back again, "Yessss, damn! It's all yours." I couldn't help but to bite my bottom lip and grunt. Just when I told her I was about to cum, her son started crying. I heard her whisper under her breath, "Fucking bullshit." She continued though, reluctant to stop. I could hear his boo-hooing draw closer. I whispered, "Yo, he's coming." However, she just ignored me.

I assumed he wouldn't come into the dining area since the lights were out. I bet wrong. He appeared right by the couch crying and looking in our direction. My jaw dropped and all I could do was tap her. By now my mind was no longer focused on reaching my orgasm. I was worried about getting caught. I tapped Skylar again, wondering how she could continue fucking with her son right there crying. As quick as I turned away, he appeared right next to us. I froze... thinking that if I stayed still he wouldn't notice me since it was dark and he woke up confused.

Skylar simply lifted her head up to glance at him and say, "Go lay down." She shoved him towards the living room, refusing to stop. I was shocked and frankly, turned off by her actions. I started to push her up to force her to stop. I knew she was frustrated as she put her panties on and stomped away. Skylar scooped her son up and demanded he go back to sleep. My intentions were not to spend the night but because I wanted more ass, I was willing to make the sacrifice. Once her son returned to his bed, we went to sleep.

I got a quickie in the morning and left. It was nothing serious like the night before because she was still mad at me. She needed to take care of her son and refusing to meet his needs was a turn off for me. We can't win them all.

Confession 6

On a few occasions I indulged in a range of unusual sexual behaviors. Some females enjoyed being liberal when it came to sex. They were exploratory and open to new things. I felt the same. I have never been ashamed or embarrassed of my sexual preferences. So when I find a female that I feel is sexually mature, I will not hold back. I have no problem exposing my sexual pleasures with those I feel are worthy. Ice, whipped cream, candle wax, sex toys, fruits, K.Y. jelly, and so forth... just to mention a few I have experimented with. I was so open to the point that I let a chick play with my butthole. That shit felt good. DON'T JUDGE ME!

Isadora was one of the first females I had met who was determined to "do me" after only seeing a picture of me. I didn't believe it but my cousin assured me that she was dead serious. When we finally met, we couldn't resist each other. Even on our first sexual encounter I held nothing back. I would've tried damn near anything with Isadora and, if given more time, I would've done more. If it wasn't for the distance between us, I definitely would have pursued a sexual relationship. I may have even considered committing.

On our first weekend together we indulged. It is a priceless memory. I was infatuated with how she was so full of life and held such a high sex drive. Isadora was exactly what I was looking for, but also I couldn't have. That left me very disappointed. I couldn't understand what it was about her either. Actually, she had a man and remained determined to get with me. I wasn't going to be the one to stop her. Knowing this caused me excitement. To this day, I still think about Isadora and that weekend we shared together. She was definitely a unique female and I doubt I'd find another like her. Had she not had a man I probably would've considered a commitment, I would have packed up and moved out there to be with her. Though that chance never presented itself due to my own activities. I am glad that I had opportunity to experience such a blissful weekend.

Then there was Janis. She presented herself respectfully so I never thought she'd get too freaky. She became a victim of my deviant sex schemes by sheer circumstance thanks to her cousin Jamiya. I was always attracted to Janis. I'd flirt with her every now and then. Yet, what she was looking for in a man, I wasn't offering.

I just wanted one night. She had doubt about my ability to satisfy a woman. I had to show her otherwise.

We shared a respect for one another. I felt comfortable enough to be open with her, so I decided to try. One particular night I proved to her how good I could be. I love a female who can appreciate and embrace my open-ness. I think it makes the experience that much better. However, every time I find a woman like myself, I tend to get caught up. I'm good at accepting things for what they are though. In that aspect, it made it easier for me to walk away when I found myself wanting more.

Timing is everything. With my luck though, I seem to meet the right type at the wrong time. I actually believed I was not meant to be a one-woman man at one point in time. I came to realize that accepting things for what they were came with benefits. Unlike all those so called playa's who can't handle a female who puts it down on a dude yet not trying to make it the norm. Which make them more of a hater than a playa, cause they're quick to try and style on a female because she shot them down after being nice enough to break them off. I can't lie, if not for her promiscuous ways, Janis had all the qualities to be a main chick.

Blind Date '00

One day I received a call from my cousin stating that her friend wants to holla at me. At first I was puzzled because I didn't understand how that was so. I haven't seen my cousin in some time and never met her friend. That's when my cousin informed me that her girlfriend saw a picture of me in my mom's crib. During our conversation I found out that shorty's name is Isadora who was from the Bronx and Puerto Rican. I was curious which picture she saw but never the less flattered that it caught her interest. I gave my cousin the okay to give Isadora my phone number so I could speak with her.

At this time I was on parole, living upstate N.Y. and come to find out she was too. Isadora was a few hours away from where I was at but further upstate. Being that I had just gotten released from prison I wasn't in the streets a lot so I talked with her a lot of the time on the phone with her. We talked about damn near everything, our likes, dislikes, our looks, and last but not least the urgency to meet. I took it upon myself to speed our meeting process up by asking my P.O. if I could get a weekend pass. Since it was apparent that it might be too early to be asking for a weekend pass, I told my P.O. that she was my fiancé.

I mentioned what I did when we spoke and she was excited, me too. The suspense was eating me alive and I just had to meet her. She gave me the name of the hotel I would be staying at all weekend. The plans she had for me were breath taking and made me more determined to make the trip. That following week when I saw my P.O. he gave me the pass. This made both of us happy and left us with not much to talk about, yet a lot of preparations to make. We discussed the hotel fee and I took care of the bus fees along with emergency money. That weekend I was ready to go and so anxious to get out of town until I got on that bus. It felt like forever just to get to where I had to go to transfer buses.

It wasn't nothing in sight to enjoy during the ride which made it worse. The CD player wasn't nearly enough to make the bus ride enjoyable especially since I didn't bring enough CD's. When I arrived at my destination, it was some shack in the middle of nowhere. I went further upstate N.Y. to spend time with this chick I felt was worth the trip. It wasn't what I would've expected for a Greyhound/Trailways bus station. I called Iris immediately to make sure that I got off at the right stop and if so, to call me a taxi. It was a half an hour before a taxi pulled up and was headed to the hotel recommended by Iris. We had decided that she would meet me at the hotel instead of picking me up. She wanted to make sure she was looking her best and had all she needed. I didn't say anything about it and gave her the room number once I got it. The hotel was nice and our room was better than I thought. When you walked in the bathroom was to your right, the mirror was the size of the wall. It was huge.

The countertop in there was dark and light brown, it had a small tub but it was a nice size bath. The room had a large king size bed in the middle of the room, it was high and made up with white sheet and a black and white comforter with plush pillows. There was a 50-inch T.V. on the wall directly in front of the bed. There was a table to the right of the bed with two chairs and a desk with a small chair on the left side of the T.V., there was beige carpeting that had a cushiony feel to it. I was more than surprised by the interior of the hotel but for the weekend this will be more than okay.

I chose to be on the second floor. I was on the phone with her from the time I got to the hotel until I received the keys and made it to my room. The whole time I could hear her giving her roommate the play by play. I could hear her roommate say, "Come on, let's see this dude who has you buggin'." So we hung up and I waited patiently for her arrival. Only a handful of people knew I left on a road trip, so I called them to let it be known that I was fine. As I spoke with my cousin to let her know that I arrived while I unpacked my bags. I did my best to make it cozy for my weekend stay. Putting my cosmetics in the bathroom, clothes on hangers, etc... Finally I went outside of my room to smoke a cigarette being that it was a nice summer afternoon. Maybe an hour past before I received a call from Isadora. When I saw her number pop up I looked around wondering what she was going to look like. This was something blind that my cousin had set up, don't ask me now why did I go before I knew what she looked like, I guess I was thirsty.... I just got out of jail. I needed my balls to stop dragging the ground.

For some strange reason my heart was pounding from the suspense as I answered the phone. After saying, "Hello!" Isadora said, "What are you doing?" I responded, "Nothing, waiting on you." Isadora then said, "Come outside right now." Still looking in every direction to see if I noticed a car pulling in—I said, "I'm already outside, I don't see you." "I'm pulling in right about now." she said. At that moment I noticed an aqua blue Camaro pulling in. The top was down and there were two occupants smiling as they looked up at me. I returned their smile while wondering which one of them was Isadora. Then as I got a closer look it was obvious that Isadora was in the passenger seat because the driver was white.

They exchanged words as they glanced at me before Iris stepped out of the car. I couldn't believe my eyes, she was every bit of a women. Isadora had her hair pinned up, her clothes looked like they were painted on, and she had a butter pecan complexion. She wore lipstick, her pants were short with a short sleeve t-shirt, and some tennis sneakers. She had to be a 36-24-36 and about

5-foot 8-inches tall with extremely outstanding breasts. When she finally got close enough I asked her if she liked what she saw. Isadora smiled and said, "Very much—what about you?" Stopping in front of me waiting for answer which the only word that came out of my mouth was, "Yes" followed with a smile.

We hugged as we looked one another in the eyes willing and then became one as we kissed passionately. As we released one another I lead her into the room helping with her bags. She seemed pleased with the room I rented especially the king size bed. We quickly began to exchange our thoughts about what we expected and what we would have done if we were disappointed. I was surprised at her response as she was of mine and we had many laughs. Iris pulled out her phone informing me that my cousin told her to call as soon as we were together. After a long humorous conversation with my cousin Iris looked at me with a huge smile on her face. We chilled in the bed talking about all kinds of things but mostly about what's next. Now that we have gotten to this point (the meeting), where do we go from there. We both had very little to ass to that except that only time will tell. I then decided to take a shower and freshen up being that I had a long day. When I was done and exited the bathroom Iris was in bed wearing a skimpy negligee. It caused me to instantly get an erection on site. Being that I was only wearing boxers.

She giggled, I smiled and walked over to join her in the bed. What a beautiful sight Isadora was sprawled out on the king size bed. Her breast were busting out of the negligee that stopped right at the hips. Her complexion was that of butter pecan ice cream with her dark hair falling a little past her shoulders. As I climbed onto the bed I fell right into her arms and kissed her on the lips. I adjusted myself on top of her as slipped my tongue into her mouth. Before I knew it we rolled over and Isadora was now on top of me. Isadora then sat up with her palms on my chest shaking her head to get her hair out of her face. Our eyes locked and she smiled at me before pulling off her negligee. It was then that I realized she had no panties on which caused my erect dick to throb. Seeing her completely naked on top of me had me thirsty for her loving but before I could get up she stopped me. Isadora then slowly leaned forward holding my hands down and began kissing me on the neck. After a few kisses on the neck she worked her way down to my chest. She continued to work her lips and tongue all over me before play with my belly button with her tongue ring.

At the same time she's pulling on my boxers in attempt of removing them off of me. I lift up my ass so it was easier for my boxers to come off. Getting to her knees so that my boxers came completely off and throwing them to the floor, she gave me a devious grin. It was then that she lowered herself not taking her eyes off of me as she found my hard cock with her mouth. With her hand holding my dick steady she put her tongue ring to work. Her mouth felt so good on the tip of my penis and the way she used her tongue ring made it even better. I grunted, my toes stiffened and I was at her mercy for what felt like too long. Feeling anxious to touch her to; I suggested we change positions so I could pleasure her simultaneously.

Which she was more than happy to oblige, turning her body so that her pussy was in my face. I then grabbed her ass with both hands parting her pussy lips with my thumbs. Lifting my head a little as I pulled her down to me and my tongue found her g-spot. It was while I was sucking on her clit I felt her hand wrap around the shaft of my cock. The harder I sucked on her, the harder Isadora jerked on my dick. When I let up on Isadora then she'd begin to put her tongue ring to work. As we took turns pleasuring one another our moans and pants matched to orgasmic feeling we both shared. I started to feel warm inside and I felt my body start to relax it was like I could of passed out right there from feeling so good. Finally the moment of truth came and we changed positions and she turned her body around where she was facing me and I looked into her eyes and kissed her and asked was she ready for me.

In a whisper she let me know she wanted me to enter her. She was laying there with her legs open and I came in between them like a thief, quick and quiet and kissed her on her stomach all the way up between her breasts. I kissed each one of her nipples before I kissed her on the lips. I was on one elbow and I used the other hand to guide the tip of my dick to her pussy and lightly pushed. I used my right knee to push up and open her left leg so that I could get all the way in there. I proceed to push slow, inching myself in, she was so warm inside. This warm feeling came over me like I was being submerged in warm water. I felt weak but not in a bad way, I was letting myself go and enjoying the sensations I was getting from Isadora. She wrapped her warm legs around my body and the heat that was coming from her was unbelievable. She was rubbing her warm hands down my back as I eased myself inside of her.

Isadora slid one of hands down between me and her to open her pussy up for me to really dig deep. It was like I felt a suction cup peel from the side of dick as it eased its way down into Isadora's pussy. I started to stroke Isadora with so much conviction as I admired how tight her pussy was. She used her other hand to roll my balls around and I got harder and harder as her legs spread wider for me. When our eyes met she appeared to be high off drugs. I leaned into her for a kiss while rubbing the side of her face and putting my hand behind her neck. I needed to make sure I was getting all the way up in there not wanting the feeling to end. I slowed down a little to not cum so fast and to make sure she was ok and to savor the moment.

I became completely still from the waist down as we kissed passionately. I then pushed myself up from her and watched her face as I worked my hips in a circular motion. For a minute there almost lost my eyes in the back of my head. When I finally got my focus back Isadora's eyes were wide open and she was watching my dick stir around in her pussy like a bowl of soup. I continued to watch Isadora as I pounded my dick repeatedly into her moist pussy causing her to moan loudly. I slowed down enough to reposition her legs, throwing them over my shoulders. Now I begun to thrust my cock in and out of Isadora's pussy. I could hear my balls and thighs smack up against her ass with every thrust. Following her lead I switched speeds and tempo frequently as we talked dirty to one another.

Being dominated in this position Isadora chose to switch positions again. This time she wanted me on my back so could be in a dominating position. As she climbed on top of me, I came to rest on my elbows. I wanted to watch as my dick slid into her juicy pussy. I waited until my chocolate rod was completely dipped into that butter pecan cream of hers before I dropped back. Isadora would use my chest to push herself up nice and slow, then free fall back down on top of me. With every free fall I would push my dick up to make sure she receives all of me. This caused her eyes to open wide and jaw to drop with a look on her face of surprise. Isadora also occasionally leaned forward so I could suck and bite on her enormous breast. That's when she would work her hips like she was using a hula hoop. I couldn't help but to moan, grunt, and scream as I exploded inside of her love tunnel.

When Isadora finally erupted she was riding me like a Cadillac on 22's hard and fast while heavily grunting. I joined in with loud groans and grunts until she just stopped moving. We looked each other in the eyes as she leaned in for a passionate kiss before resting on top of me. I never pulled out of her I remained inside of her as we laid there holding each other. It was going to be a very passionate weekend with no disturbance. That night we stood outside, the nice summer breeze against our bare skin while smoking a cigarette. The whole weekend was filled with hot passionate sex, smoking, drinking, and laughter. It was a welcome home weekend that I could never forget.

Icy & Hot '00–'01

It's crazy how one thing can lead to another, and before you know it you're doing something you didn't have planned. That's the case with this female named Janis. That last thing I thought was that Janis and I would end up fucking. I enjoyed flirting with her and really wasn't pressed to hit it. Janis definitely was a fine Latin woman with nigga's lined up doing whatever. She was around 5-foot 4-inches tall, wide hips, fat ass and nice size breasts. Janis was about her business, yet very promiscuous. She and I always were good peoples and at the time I was sharing an apartment with her cousin.

Her cousin named Jamiya had been my roommate for some time and told people she was my sister. At this time Jamiya was stripping and occasionally dabbled with cocaine. I wasn't thrilled about her ways but I wasn't going to turn my back on her neither. I was extremely tough on her especially with what went on under our roof. I never understand what went through Jamiya's mind. Still I cared enough not to let her just hurt herself, so I never passed judgment. It was one weekend when Jamiya was emotionally distraught and wanted to go get fucked up. She was talking all crazy and shit which made me worried. I refused to let her go out alone in her unstable condition, and not with just anybody. She threatened to call Janis and I felt that was the wrong person to threaten me with. Out of everybody I knew Janis would understand why I was being hard on Jamiya. Jamiya told Janis that I wouldn't let her leave the house but didn't mention why. Afterwards she passed me the phone like Janis could change my mind. I told Janis just to get her ass over to the house before her cousin does something stupid. I refused to go into detail over the phone and told her I would explain it when she got there. Once Janis arrived Jamiya tried to hurry up and get out of the house before I could explain anything to Janis. Janis on the other hand refused to go anywhere until she knew what was going on.

Things got really intense as I explained my position to Janis and we addressed Jamiya. We all agreed that Janis should stick around because Jamiya seemed determined to get her some cocaine. We finally convinced Jamiya to chill in the crib and call my homeboy John that she liked over. I suggested that we smoke and drink with her until my homeboy got there. He was the only dude that I didn't mind coming to the crib. Jamiya and I had the no guy, no girl rule in effect for privacy reasons but John was an exception. Janis took Jamiya to the liquor store to get whatever she wanted to drink. When they returned they had all types of liquor plus a bag of ice. There was a bottle of 99 Banana's, Hennessy, Parrot Bay, and a bottle of Bacardi Lémon. We were about to be fucked up. I gave Janis this look of disappointment and she said, "It was either this or that other shit." I needed some Uncle Pauly, it was going to be a long night. After she said that, I was just happy that Jamiya was staying in the house. I also realized it was going to be a long night if I didn't get out of the house. Jamiya was already taking shots of liquor and blasting the radio.

I could see that she was taking advantage of this situation. Janis wasn't a real drinker nor did she smoke, so for her it was a babysitting job. I, on the other hand had to drink and smoke just because of how this night was looking. Jamiya refused to get comfortable unless Janis agreed to do the same. It was obvious that if Janis attempted to leave before John arrived, Jamiya would do the same. Being that John had no clue of what was going on, he didn't rush right over. It took John three hours to get there. I still was trying to get out of the house when Janis said, "If you leave I'm leaving too." I said, "She wanted you and John to stay, so there is no need for me to stay." Knowing that I was right she insisted I don't do her like that. Yet I just prepared for my departure as Janis walked off.

I was trying to get some pussy and Janis didn't show any interest. This was all the more reason for me to go out instead of staying in. Then as I was about to head out I heard Jamiya saying, "and where do you think your going brother!?" When I turned to face her, I saw Janis behind her smiling. "I'm going to take care of some business sis." I said trying to keep a straight face. I then gave Janis the evil eye hoping she just let me be. Which was simply ignored because Janis screamed out, "He's lying, Jamiya." Looking past Jenna I could see Janis just grinning and laughing silently. When Jenna regained my attention she just stood there with a disappointed look on her face. It wasn't until Jenna said, "If you're going out then I'm going out too and you already know what I'm trying to do." I stared at her in disbelief yet I know she's capable of doing just that especially if Janis left as well. I then looked at Janis and said, "That's that bullshit you did." Then without looking at Jamiya and walking pass the both of them I said, "Alright sis I'm chilling." John was in the living room listening to music clueless to what's really going on. I headed to the kitchen because I needed a strong drink plus I wanted to roll a blunt.

After a few drinks and a couple of laughs we decided to just sit back and enjoy a movie. Jamiya chose to put on Cruel Intentions which fit Jamiya perfectly considering the title. I took a seat next to Janis who looking good and sexy wearing one of Jamiya's long pajama shirts. The shirt came down to Janis's thick thighs and suddenly I had my own cruel intention. John was sitting on the other end enjoying all the attention Jamiya was giving him. So being that Janis played a big part in why I was still there, I chose to see why. I said, "So what's up Janis, are you and I finally gonna, you know?" As I probed her body. Her response was breath taking and mind boggling. Janis looked at me with disappointment and said, "I heard about you sweetie and I'll pass." Hearing that made my jaw drop leaving my mouth open, I couldn't believe what I was hearing. Before I could respond Jamiya said, "Janis what did you hear?" "Yeah, what did you hear and from who?" I said. Janis was startled, not by the questions but by one of them coming from Jamiya. She must have thought that Jamiya didn't hear our conversation, because I had thought the same thing. Still Janis hesitated before saying, "Who do you think could have told me?" I paused for a good minute thinking of who could have told her anything about me. Then it hit me and I couldn't believe it, I blurted out, "Emilia is the one who told you that, didn't she?"

By the look on Janis's face I knew I had guessed right. Being that Jamiya had no clue who Emilia was made her more interested. I couldn't help but smile as I became more curious to hear what Emilia said. The whole time John just sat and seemed to enjoy this group conversation. Janis then said, "She said, that you aren't that good in bed." I could not help but smile before saying in a laughing tone, "Don't believe everything you hear, especially from someone who did anything I asked." Jamiya shocked me by saying, "My brother will do you right, I bet. Don't believe that bitch." With all that being said we returned to watching the movie but now I was more determined to show Janis that I wanted her back to hurt and her stomach to be in her chest. While Janis watched T.V. I whispered to her, "Different strokes for different folks." "You're real cute, huh?" she responded in a seductively low voice. I succeeded in making her smile and wasn't going to stop there. Out of nowhere Jamiya said, "That's right bro, get at that." It was almost like Janis wasn't her cousin but instead some chick. Yet we simultaneously said, "You're too fucking much, a hot mess." I got up to go fix me another drink and asked if anybody wanted one. Nobody requested one so I returned with my Hennessy on the rocks, which suddenly gave me an idea.

I killed my double shot and placed a piece of ice in my mouth. I then leaned over to Janis like I was going to tell her something. Before she realized I wasn't going to say anything, I kissed her on the neck below her ear. She flinched in surprise and looked at me with a smirk on her face. "What you know about ice?" is what she said after I revealed it to her. Letting the ice fall back into the glass I said, "More than you think." "Why are you playing with me?" Janis said. In turn I responded by saying, "Why are you playing yourself?" Before she could gather something to say back to me Jamiya screamed out, "You know you want to, you need to stop fronting." "Matter of fact, let's see who uses ice better?"

Jamiya was fucked up more than I was and Janis and John were just a little tipsy. Still Jamiya's idea caught everybody's attention especially mines. Finally after a little persuasion Janis who was the only one fronting, agreed. The only thing was, Jamiya and John weren't allowed to be in the same room. So Jamiya went and retrieved a cup of ice before disappearing into her room with John. I had also retrieved a bowl of ice at the same time as Jamiya. While we were in the kitchen Jamiya said to me, "Bro, you better put it on her, don't make us look bad." She then kissed me on the cheek and skipped out of the kitchen giggling.

Finally we were alone in the living room and I couldn't wait to get a hold of Janis. Standing up looking down at her I said, "Are you ready to find out if Emilia was telling you the truth?" She looked at me with a smirk on her face and said, "I see you're not gonna just sit and watch this movie with me?" Putting a piece of ice in my mouth and placing the bowl on the floor, I shook my head no. Then sliding the ice out between my lips and grabbing it with two fingers I said, "Do you really want to watch T.V.?" Before she could answer I started sucking on the ice and catching the drips with my tongue. I could see she was intrigued by my actions which left her speechless. I repeated the question as the ice melted and retrieved another piece. This time it was Jamiya voice that screamed out, "No, no she don't." I couldn't help but smile as Janis said with laughter, "Hey John, seal her mouth if you know what I mean." Now I was standing in front of her with the ice between my lips and knelt in front of her. Drops of water dripped onto her legs and with every drip she let out a sigh. "That's cold," she said as I moved closer towards her. I slowly was lifting her pajama shirt up past her waist revealing her Victoria Secrets. All along letting drops of water drip onto her bare skin.

As soon as I saw her belly button I leaned in and started kissing on it as the melting ice trickled down her pelvis. When I finally looked up at her she seemed to be staring at me in a loss of words. I then began to lovely stare at her as I pulled at her panties determined to reveal her secret. Surprisingly, she was more than willing to let her secret be revealed. Once I got her panties off I reached over to the side of me and got another piece of ice out of the cup. With the ice between my lips I started to work my way up her inner thighs as the ice melted on contact. I could feel Janis quiver from the coldness of the ice as she open the gateway to her love pool. In no time the ice was completely melted but this time I reached for the bowl without looking.

I kissed on her outer thigh as I felt for the bowl of ice that I now placed on the couch. Placing another piece of ice into my mouth I continued my way back to her wet pussy. I then let the ice caress her clit and pussy lips until it melted. This time when I lifted my head to look at her I noticed a piece of ice in her hand. Janis then placed it in my mouth and returned to playing with it on her clitoris. The temperature was definitely rising in the room. Regardless I now decided to use my tongue to splash around in the pool and bounce off of her diving board. All that bouncing and splashing around caused me to almost drown by the waterfall that was activated. Janis was uncontrollably moaning and squirming around as she grabbed hold of my head.

Realizing what had transpired I got up preparing to scuba dive in her pussy. Grabbing a diving suit I began putting it on before I plunged into her pool of hot lava. As I turned back towards her, Janis was sprawled out on the couch. I quickly dropped my pants, put on the condom and prepared to mount. I grabbed both her legs throwing them over my shoulders. I placed my knee on the inner section of the couch while keeping one foot on the floor. This gave me totally control of the situation leaving her helpless. She quickly looked up at me wide eyed, pleading with the look in her eyes "Take it easy on me." I simply smiled as I said sarcastically, "Don't worry Emilia warned you!" Then I looked down at her nicely shaved pussy. My dick was throbbing as I guided it towards her then into the deep end. I slowly descended every inch of me inside of Janis before I whispered, "Hold on tight." Having said that I began to plunge my hardness in and out of her pink hole. With every plunge Janis called out my name which only made me fuck her harder and faster. I damn near had her hanging off the sofa. Still it didn't slow me down as I grunted with every thrust not caring who heard me. Janis accepted every bit of me also sharing her satisfaction with the entire house.

We eventually broke night by the time we were done and Janis decided to go home. There was silence between us for a long period of time. She would just look at me and smile, shaking her head, which left me wondering. Yet before I could get the question out of my mouth, I heard Jamiya, "Was that my brother making you holla?" Janis just broke out laughing as she said, "Shut up stupid, anyway I'm about to leave, call me later." "That's what I am talking about bro, and I'll call you miss, later!" Jamiya said. I then walked Janis to the door and we paused to take in the early morning air. After a moment or two we looked at one another, kissed one last time before she headed down the steps. I stood in the doorway watching her walk to her car when she turned to me and said, "Thank You."

All in the Family

I for one believe that a single person is allowed to sleep with whomever he or she pleases. I have always found it shocking when I mess with a female and her family members chooses to pursue me. Don't get me wrong I never turned away from an opportunity like that. If they are good with crossing that fine line, then who am I to question it or expose their desire to pleasure me. I won't act on it if it will cause me a potential headache in the long run. Things have definitely changed a lot since I was younger and in school. Being in a relationship with a girl regardless of time put you on the off limits list. Today they don't give a shit, if you look good and they want you, they not going to stop until they get you. Only to say the dick was good and I am taking her man, or that shit was whack and I don't know why I wasted my time.

The friends weren't allowed to fuck with you let alone a family member. Even the neighborhood slut would be skeptical depending on the male or female it was. Nowadays everyone is fair game and there is no respect for one another. I have had my share of families and can't understand how they can be around each other like everything is everything. It crazy yet weird to see them act as if it's nothing especially since there's only one that will step out there and flirt with me just to rub it in the others noses. But I guess it doesn't matter, especially since nobody has the right to even get upset, they were in my eyes just set test dummies/lab rats.

How good was their pussy? Was it as good as that person looks or dresses? You become fascinated with people and it turns into lust and that's how so many women fuck all these dudes and vice versa. It's nothing more that, I was going through a scientific phase in which I'd put every female who crossed my path was tested. An interesting phase yet once it's over it's like you don't even know them and lost all the attraction you thought you had for the person. That's how you know it was a toot it and boot it deal. Where is the family bond, the family morals, or values or the loyalty amongst each other? It's this type of behavior that makes it hard to be considered trustworthy. It makes it hard to commit to a monogamous relationship. That also goes to say if the roles were reversed.

Sleeping with members of my shorty's family was fair game if the relationship wasn't based on love. If anything, I tried to find out which ones where down to let me hit it (have sex). These types of behaviors also makes it easier to understand why they say "Bitches ain't shit" and "Hoes and Nigga's are dogs." I have also come to realize what separates a nigga from a man and a bitch from a women. Those distinctions are: having some self-respect, by have some admiration for yourself, approval of oneself, having a healthy self-esteem, being comfortable in your own skin, self-control with your choices in life, self-discipline, know when to say no, self-sufficient be able to take care of yourself and your family... not looking for a hand out or someone to take care of you, self-righteous you have to have some morals and values that you live by. Having one without the other doesn't help much and I learned that the hard way.

Karissa was a female I met when I was behaving like a dog. I noticed her paying extra attention to me and decided to holla. It wasn't until I caught her and her sister walking past my crib. Seizing the moment to exchange numbers with Karissa. I gave her an open invitation to chill. Karissa was similar to a Wendy's frosty, bitter chocolate complexion and thick. She was very thick and pretty. I may have spoken with her a few times on the phone before we actually hooked up. During which, I found out that she had a baby and still involved with the baby's father. Still she showed great interest in hooking up, and really didn't care about her situation. So when she called talking about she wanted to get together, I invited her over.

It was a crib my cousin had that he moved out of and we kept as the BOOM-BOOM room. Which means that it had very little furniture, maybe a kitchen table set, an air mattress and some dishes. The bathroom was the only room that wasn't stripped of anything major. It really didn't bother me being that the crib wasn't her primary objective, I was. I guaranteed her that she wouldn't have to worry about anybody seeing her. That the crib was on the low and that I wasn't going to let her get caught-up. When she arrived at the BOOM-BOOM room, she was startled when she saw we weren't alone.

I didn't think anything of it because my cousin and his shorty don't run they mouths. After explaining that to her while we smoked, she began to relax. Once the weed was gone and we had a few laughs, I took Karissa into the bathroom. My cousin was already in the room with the air-mattress and the bathroom was the only other room with a door. I closed the door behind us and said, "Finally I got you all to myself." "So what you going to do with me?" explained Karissa. Pressing her up against the wall I kissed her on the lips letting my tongue invade her mouth. As we kissed I found myself palming her ass and caressing her breasts. Moments later I was unbuckling Karissa's belt, and unbuttoning her pants.

During all of that she slipped out one question. "Do you have a condom?" Reaching into my pocket and pulling one out, there was no stopping me from dicking her down. With nothing else being said, we stripped. As I slipped on the condom, I watched as Karissa pulled her pants down and freed one of her legs. I on the other hand stepped completely out of my pants, boxers, and sneakers. The bathroom was narrow and long with the door at the opposite end of the sink and toilet. The shower was off to the right as soon as you enter, and a window was off to the left of the toilet. The sink was off to the right of the toilet with a medicine cabinet over it. One thing was that the door didn't have a lock on it which slipped my mind at the time.

Still I had her by the window standing up against the wall contemplating how it was going to go down. In the mean time I was fondling her vagina with the head of my dick as I sucked on her neck. I could hear her panting as I slide the tip between her pussy lips. Finally without warning I spun her around and threw her up against the wall. Without being instructed to do so, Karissa assumed the position pushing her ass out to me. With her hands flat against the wall and legs spread she looked at me saying, "I'm waiting." I stepped between her legs and holding my dick by the shaft, I proceeded to penetrate her chia-pet. I was practically on my toes as I used unnecessary force causing her to moan. Being that we weren't alone she muffled the moans which must of led my cousin to believe nothing was happening. That's because as I was slapping my dick into her now wet pussy the door opened.

We both froze up for what felt like too long. Me looking at him and vice-versa. Karissa kept her face down, not jumping, not moving one inch. My cousin smiling quickly apologized as he backed out closing the door. I had my cock inside of her hole with my palms on her ass cheeks. I gave him a smile on his way out and once he was gone we resumed where we left off. We refused to stop until we both squeezed out that creamy liquid that makes us all happy and on cloud nine. Being that she had a little baby and a jealous man I decided not to pursue anymore rendezvous. The next time I saw Karissa, she was dealing with a friend of mines. It probably was a shock to her when she realized he was leaving with me. He wasn't aware of our past and we never bother to tell him.

It wasn't until I was at the bar with a friend who messed with Iesha, sister, that I met her cousin. Summer is what I later on found out was her name. That's was when I stepped to them to say, Hi to Karissa's sister, who introduced us. Summer had to be about 5-foot 10 to 5-foot 11 inches tall and thick all over with a pretty face. I thought nothing of it due to the fact that I messed with her cousin and thought it be wrong. Which I soon came to find out wasn't the case and she had inquired about me. They already had this in the works to just pass my ass around I see. Well I was going to enjoy sense they wanted to do this, I was going to take full advantage. Still I didn't press the issue and then two weekends later at the same bar Summer pressed the issue about getting up with each other. I was shocked and flattered when she walked up to me and said, "Don't make any plans to leave with anybody tonight." Looking her in the eyes with a smirk on my face, I said, "Why do you have plans for me?" It was obvious that she was looking forward to creeping with me. Still I played dumb and she responded, "Yeah, you're going home with me." With no hesitation I said, "Whenever you're ready, so am I, so don't front I' am not about that life." "I just hope you can hang, your ass better be ready for this pounding about to lay on you."

Mind you, Summer and Ellen were there with Karissa and they all seemed to be enjoying themselves. My man Biz was there but my boy who messed with Karissa wasn't. Biz and I played pool while the ladies got drunk and danced to the music. After some time Summer let me know she was ready to leave. I then informed Biz on what was going down, he decided to leave with us. It was then that Summer let me know that she was dropping her cousin's off first. Biz decided that he would have her take him home as well, hoping to convince Ellen to join him. We jumped in the back seat putting Karissa in the middle while Ellen rode shotgun.

The music muffled all the laughing Summer and Ellen was doing as we drove off. Karissa was drunk and just happy to have been out for a change. She tried to make small talk but all I could do was smile, I was twisted. For a brief moment I could see us fucking again and if I knew better I'd say she did too. I made one or two small jokes and left it alone before I'd say something I had no business saying. Once she got rid of everybody, she couldn't wait to get me home. Luckily the last drop was around the corner from her crib which surprised me. The whole time I wondered if she knew about me and her cousin. I mean I assumed she didn't but then again it wasn't like she really gave a fuck. She was determined to get me in the bed one way or another. She wanted to feel this dick and I was ready to give it to her. One thing for certain Summer wasn't a little girl and I had to do my best performance in that bed. I admit I was a little intimidated by her thick muscular body but that made me more determined to handle her ass.

Showing me in, Summer demanded I go into the living room for a minute. Closing the door behind her and shooting upstairs she said, "I don't stay here much so my room is a mess." I yelled out to her, "Who cares as long as the bed is clean." I mean really it's like three in the morning, I thought to myself. A couple minutes pass before she said, "Alright, you can come up now." Finally reaching her room I realized she wasn't lying about not staying there, her blinds wasn't even up in her room. Her dresser wasn't completely assembled nor was the headboard to her bed. Another thing is that Summer was in the bathroom freshening up. I screamed out to her, "You mind if I get comfortable?" That's after I had already started stripping placing the condom on the night stand. "You need to because I' am," she said.

Laying on her bed in my boxers I admired how the street lights lit up her room just enough to admire this sexual experience. Suddenly, Summer appeared wearing nothing but a tee shirt that stopped at her hips. Standing at the door Summer said, "You aren't comfortable yet?" I said to her, "Yes, can't you tell?" Noticing her staring at my boxers she shook her head saying, "Nope, you look uncomfortable to me." Without hesitation I took off my boxers as Summer looked on with a smile on her face. "That's more like it." As he headed towards me taking off her t-shirt. As I laid there watching her shirt come off I thought: Did I bite off more than I could chew. Summer was Serena W. built and a bit thicker in some areas making a brother look malnourished. I decided to climb this mountain and leave my mark. Back shots seemed to be the most favorable position and secondly on her back with her feet on my shoulders. I became Summer's weekend special for the next few weeks. Then one weekend I was chilling and decided to go get in a few games of pool at the bar. After a few games and a couple drinks, Summer, Ellen, and Shivani walked in. We all greeted one another before they took their place at a table in the corner. From their table they could see the pool table with no problem. That is if nobody is standing in between them and the pool table. Me being somewhat of a pool shark, I was playing games for either a drink or they would have to give me $5.00.

So when Shivani came to the table and placed her quarters down I couldn't help but smile. She had no idea who she thought she was playing against; I am the champion. I informed her that in order to play she'd have to play for drinks or cash. Shivani then looked at me and said, "I can get any drink I want?" I smiled at her question. I had to scratch my eye brow for a brief minute because she really thought she was going to beat me at MY game. "Shit, you're buying so knock yourself out." I had a thing for Summer and she knew it so she put up a big front like

I wasn't on her level. Summer was drop dead gorgeous to anybody who didn't know her and a dime to those who did. Which
kind of made it hard to believe that she was related to Summer,
Ellen, and Karissa. She had this Swiss almond complexion, long
rust colored hair that came down to her shoulders which was very
curly. She stood about 5-foot 5-inches to 5-foot-6 inches tall and
around 120 pounds give or take. Shivani had this Alicia Keys style
of dressing which complimented her beauty.

Then to top it all off, Summer had a mean pool game which
she made sure I realized. There was flirting involved but too
direct which seemed to separate me from the rest. I chose to use
pool to get to know her better, being it was obvious we both
liked playing it. We both hated losing and determined to prove
who was better at pool. I took that opportunity to invite her to
go out to a billiards to play with no interruptions. She accepted
and we exchange numbers on the low, that way nobody knew. At
least nobody outside of our immediate circle, I just hoped Summer wouldn't hate. The first time we chilled she asked did I mess
with any of her cousin's and I said, "Yes." I admitted to messing
with Karissa but mentioned nothing about Summer.

I guess since Karissa was my boys' baby momma it didn't bother
Bonnie at all. That night I took her to a nice billiard that sold drinks
and wasn't in the hood. We had a great time, we joked around and
flirted as we drank the night away. Afterwards I dropped him off
at her home nothing more, nothing less. I made no suggestion to
go out again nor did I hint that I would be calling her. I figured

I'd opened the door enough and it's up to her to come in. A few days passed before I received a call from Shivani. Which I was glad that she did because I enjoyed her company and was hoping she'd occupy some of my time. She suggested that we hang out that same night if I wasn't too busy. I agreed with Shivani and made plans to pick her up around ten o'clock. I was running late and when I arrived in front of her house, I decided to call her. When she answered the first words out of her mouth were, "You're calling to cancel on me?" "Are you asking or telling me?" I asked. Before Shivani could respond I said, "Better yet how about you come outside and repeat that?" Moments later the house door opened and she appeared in the doorway.

Without saying another word we hung up our cell phones and she headed towards the car. Shivani got into the car and was smiling and said, "You're not funny!" I just smiled and waited for her to get settled in before I turned the music back up. As she finished adjusting herself I slowly begun to pull off. She then asked, "Where are we going? If you don't mind me asking?" I then asked, "I don't know, maybe to have a few drinks and play pool." "That sounds like a good enough plan to me." Shivani said. I then turned up the music sat back and headed for a crib I was sharing with my homeboy. It was like the home away from home for me and my homeboy. It was only fifteen minutes away from where Shivani lived but out of the way for uninvited guests.

When we reached the crib I suggested to Shivani to follow me inside. I kind of figured that she believed we were going out to a bar. Which made it more interesting to see what she thought of my crib or should I say our crib. As I put the key in the door and started to turn it, I said to Shivani, "I just want to let you know this is our final destination." With that being said, I opened the door and she followed me inside. I turned to her to watch the expression on her face as I slowly closed the front door. I simply smiled when she looked at me and said, "This is definitely what's up!" She went on to say, "I can't believe you bother going to the bar."

As soon as you enter the pool table is right in the center of the so-called living room. Straight ahead past that is one couch which faces the door, unless we decide to put it sideway to watch television—due to the fact that the 44-inch plasma was mounted right over the couch. It was more for the people playing pool or poker more so than it was for those sitting on the couch. To the left of the pool table was a wall with a small bulletin board. The front door opened into the crib and when closed in the left hand corner was a laptop and all in one printer.

Right off the living room is the small kitchen area and right on top of the fridge is the liquor. Inside of the fridge is the shelf for water, one for V8's, and one for Smirnoff ice—all flavors. Shivani never made it into any other part of the apartment except the bathroom. Just for the record one room had nothing but a T.V. and a sofa. The other room was occupied by two pit bulls and the back of the apartment. I had the television on with a DVD playing and just the table lights on. Shivani rolled up the haze while I made the drinks, she refused to drink any Smirnoff ice. So as we sipped on some Hennessy w/coke and smoked the Haze, we played a few games of pool. Afterwards we decided to just enjoy the comfort of the couch and plasma. I threw in another movie before joining Shivani on the couch.

"I enjoyed chilling with you tonight," Shivani said as she pulled me towards her. "I'm glad you enjoyed yourself, I aim to please," as I was leaning in to kiss her. Laying her down across the couch, we kissed and caressed one another. It was a matter of minutes before I had all of her clothes off and was admiring her body. The weird thing was I hadn't made any attempt to strip, instead I began to kiss her all over. I was feeling nice and wanted to just please instead of just being pleased, which wasn't often. I started by kissing her on the lips, then her neck, made my way to her breast before working my way to her belly button. When I reached her pelvis I paused to look at her face, noticing how pleased Shivani was. Her butter pecan complexion and soft skin had men anxious to taste her juices. Her pussy was bikini waxed and as pretty as she is. I then placed one of her legs over the back of the couch before positioning myself for a taste of Shivani.

I parted her vaginal lips with my thumbs before allowing my tongue to gently massage Shivani's clit. Which shortly went from a gentle massage to a combination of nibbling and sucking. Shivani was moaning and squirming out of control causing me to suck harder on her clitoris. I refuse to stop until I made her climax and lose control of her body. I have to admit it was unusual of me not to be pressed to hit it. Still was my pleasure and I enjoyed myself the way I wanted too. I still show respect to each of these women because there never was any controversy. We all were able to be around one another without being uncomfortable. I then realized that some families have very little respect for one another, let alone themselves. How can you dare trust others if you can't trust family or yourself? Where are the family morals and values when honesty, trust, and loyalty has no place? I wasn't any better because I criticize their behavior but still indulged myself. Yet at the time I was the shit amongst those in my immediate circle, and I wasn't shit to those on the outside or to myself.

Confession 7

It's safe to say from experience that there are women/females who are emotionally committed to one man. Yet still chose to be sexually active with other males and females. It's hard to believe but you can't love a person if you're willing to cheat on them. Self-satisfaction is what many truly love which includes lack of respect and loyalty to and or for others. To say you love someone but have no respect for their feelings is an oxymoron. Although there are people who love the idea of being in a relationship. Of knowing there is someone home waiting for them regardless of how good the relationship itself is? Then you have those who allow their partner to do whatever for the love of their partner. That is until the opportunity arises where they get to return the favor.

It's what I consider—The Safety Net—which allows a person to enjoy the pleasures of many, meanwhile only cater to Mr. and Mrs. Exclusive. At one point and time I sought out these types of females. I took great pride in pleasing these females whether it be mental or physical. Which in most cases mental pleasure leads to physical pleasure. At times it caused me some emotional discomfort and even some mental anguish. Still it was the game I chose to play and I learned to accept what came with it. Please believe that the acceptance part was the hardest part of the game I choose. Nevaeh was the respectable woman who went to college and worked. She also was in a long-term relationship but seemed to be unhappy. Besides work and school her life seemed to be at a standstill, at least that's what I thought. We talked a lot and we got to know one another extremely well. We shared educational, emotional, humorous, and sexual conversations with each other. I never minded holding a conversation or taking time out of my day to chill with Nevaeh. She was very mature and had a sensible outlook on my ways and actions. I have to admit that Nevaeh was the very first female I experienced a friendship of this magnitude. I actually cared for Nevaeh and respect her decision to move on. She always will be close in heart and have my best wishes in all that she does.

Breanna on the other hand chose to be very promiscuous while her fiancé was in jail. She took care of him throughout his incarceration but couldn't control her sexual urges. Still she let it be known that her heart belongs to her fiancé at the end of the day.

Breanna was mature, smart and knew how to get what she wants when she wanted it. Her priorities were in order and I could communicate with her on any level. Unlike Nevaeh, Breanna was infatuated with the street life, except for the violence. Our friendship was very brief and served its purpose, although I came up short. Still I have to say Breanna was a unique and a respectable female. For whatever their reasons were for doing what they did and how they did it, wasn't my concern. At the end of the day I was glad they chose me to do it with.

I was fond of how they presented themselves not only to me but to anyone they encountered. Everything about them was average. Given the circumstance involved I would probably have attempted to pursue a more serious relationship. Not to mention I was so far from committing to a female that it really didn't matter. We all knew what to expect regardless of how any of us truly felt.

Hit and Run '00–'01

She was a young attractive female who worked and attended school, college to be exact. Her name is Nevaeh and she had a nice figure with a caramel complexion. Nevaeh had a good head on her shoulders, a remarkable attitude and a good sense of humor. I couldn't help but try my luck with her but she informed me about her current relationship. I respected her honesty but decided to test her loyalty to her man. Not to mention her job was in the area so I couldn't help but drop in on her. Plus her supervisor was a friend of mines which also worked in my favor. So I would stop in on their lunch break or just after shift change. Whether it was both of them there or just Nevaeh, we use to kick it.

I even would bring them something to eat if they asked me too. Being that I was running the streets, I took this time to free myself from all that comes with running the streets. They also enjoyed the company because it helped their day go by quicker. Plus it was impossible to chill with them outside of work. Especially Nevaeh who the only other time I'd be able to see her, would be at the club with her man. Even then I would use Joan, her supervisor to get close to her. We kind of had this thing where we flirted with one another, mostly for fun. Nevaeh was completely aware of me having numerous sexual partners on a casual basis. Being that she worked at a hotel I frequently used. I limited myself to only a chosen few females Nevaeh was allowed to see.

Still when at the club I'd be on my "I am leaving with somebody's shorty" shit. We had built a friendship where we were like best buddies and could talk about anything. Since Nevaeh had a man, I flirted with all the pretty employees except Joan. None of them seemed to mind my flirtations behavior, in fact I believe they enjoyed the attention. It's not like I wasn't aware of the shift change gossip. Still Nevaeh was the one I devoted my attention too, plus we bonded in a unique way. We didn't judge each other which made it a lot easier for us to be open with one another. Being promiscuous didn't give me this luxury so that made our friendship that more special.

Anyway, on this particular day I could see that something was bothering Nevaeh. So I allowed her to share what was troubling her as I sat and listened. Come to find out her man done something that made Nevaeh question her relationship. I sat and listened shocked at how she was expressing her anger. I used to tell her, if she ever felt the need to seek pleasure elsewhere don't hesitate to holla. Yet, I never thought that day would come but on this particular day, it came. Nevaeh suggested we chill out at Joan's crib after work. I was shocked at the idea of chilling at Joan's house but gladly accepted the invitation. They prepared a hot meal for a brother and that night we got better acquainted. We had a barrel of laughs, watched a movie, and discussed going somewhere we could be alone. Joan's crib wasn't good because of her children and Nevaeh refused to go to a hotel.

Which I didn't blame her because somebody always sees you coming from a hotel. It always seems to be like that when a person is creeping or sneaking around. The last thing I wanted was for Nevaeh's man to find out, for her sake. Although he had to do something real stupid to push her into the arms of another man. Especially since his girl worked at a hotel and he knew we practically lived there. Which gave her a variety of men to choose from and he goes and fucks up. Very naïve of him to believe she would not turn to someone else if he kept fucking up. This Nevaeh shared with me and John as we drank and smoked that night. I shared my appreciation for being the one she chose to creep with.

Joan sat back enjoying every moment especially when Neicy said, "I hope you can handle me?" Joan butted in with, "You know I'm gonna hear about it," walking away laughing. I looked at both of them and fixed my eyes on Nevaeh and said, "I guess you better pick the day and time you want me to handle you." Still I chose not to talk shit which they expected me to do. I just chilled out finding humor in their sarcastic remarks until it was time for us to go. I left first not wanting to be there when Nevaeh's man arrived. The next day when I seen her at work it was interesting. Being that we finally chilled we were more outspoken towards one another. Our friendship had elevated just a little which left us with a burning desire. We mentally teased ourselves with talk of sexual acts of interest.

She took the time to inform me that later that week, we'd be hooking up. I was to be meeting her at Joan's house and from there we were off. It was that Wednesday when I received a call from Nevaeh telling me to meet her at 11:30 a.m., at Joan's house. I just said, "Fine, will do," and hung up the phone. When I reached the rendezvous spot I was greeted with a sneaky smile. It's my belief that she was shocked at what she was about to go do, plus how she went about doing it. To my surprise, Nevaeh had a place for us to slide off too. With that being said I figured it best if she drove to our destination. Before we left Joan's crib I asked, "Who crib are we going to?" She replied, "It's my cousin's crib and we have until 5:00 p.m. to use it." I just smiled looking at her with such infatuation. At the same time turning up the stereo and reclining in my seat. I was completely taken back by how smooth and well planned this was.

It was then that I came to believe women are better than men when it comes to creeping. My day seem to have start off very interesting and I couldn't wait to make the best of the rest of it. It probably took us like 15 to 20 minutes to get to her cousins block, crosstown. Her cousin lived on a somewhat quiet block. Considering we weren't from the block we went undetected as we made our way to her cousin's crib. It was like I was the only one unaware of what was going on. I say that because once her cousin opened the front door, they were all giggles. Then without introduction her cousin said, "Damn girl he's a cutie, that's my girl." We all broke out in laughter before I said, "Thank You! I see good looks run in your family too." Her jaw seemed to drop and she said, "And he has manners, polite, and pretty smile." She continued on, "Anymore like him? Don't hesitate to bring him by."

I finally turned to Nevaeh and said, "Your cousin is crazy." With that being said we all began laughing as Nevaeh's cousin made her way to the door. Before she left I overheard her tell Nevaeh, "Do everything I would do and a little bit more." I heard them giggling in the hallway by the door I can see I am in for a surprise. I can't wait because I been waiting to lay her down for a minute. "Get out of here, you're stupid," replied Neicy. They continued to laugh as she walked out the door. Once again I reminded Nevaeh that her cousin is crazy cool, as I toured her house. "Don't pay her any mind, would you like something to drink?" replied Neicy. "Yea some juice if she has any." It was already set in my mind I would submit to Nevaeh's demands. I just didn't share that information with Nevaeh. Before she escorted me into the bedroom, Nevaeh mentioned something about the table chair.

I then asked, "What about the chair?" She then responded, "Bring one of them into the room." I suddenly began smiling because there was some shit that was about to go down in this room that I know I am not going to be able to tell anybody. Once I brought the chair to the room, I found that Nevaeh was already undressing. She had a black zebra stripped bra and black thongs. She had a nice toned body and smooth brown skin. I could smell her Victoria Secret body butter lotion from across the room. It was time to devour, and I was definitely really to eat. I placed the chair in between the bed and the window and started to undress myself. I took off my shirt and kind of flex a little bit so she can see that I be on my workout shit. I was really trying to impress, leave something penciled on her memory before I got between them legs.

As I was showing off my chest, I looked up and seen her walking over to the chair, as she stepped you can see all the muscles in her calves more and make her butt cheeks bounce with every step. I was ready to pounce like a Lion taking out his prey. She adjusted the chair so that the back of it was against the dresser for stability purposes. The bedroom was nice and clean and very spacious. I really liked her cousin's interior decorating style. The room was two toned in color with nice nuance colors. It was a black, white, and pink room. Very different from other bedrooms I been in. The walls were white, there was a king size, plush pillow-top bed with white bedding, and a pink headboard. It was the first thing you see when you came into the room. It was against the far wall centered between the closet on the left and the window was on the right.

The curtains were white with splashes of pink and black. They looked custom made. There was this huge black painting behind the bed. I was looking around this room in awe. Her cousin had a couple dollars. There was a coffee table in the middle of the floor a few feet from the foot of the bed. It had white legs and a pink top. She had a pink love seat with white and black pillows on it. It looked like nobody has ever sat on it. With a beige and white dresser. Very classy. I think I could get use to this. By the time I was fully undressed, Nevaeh was sprawled out across the bed with her arms above her head and one leg straight and her foot propped up on the bed. She was patiently waiting for me to devour her.

Which I was more than happy to do so and climbed onto the bed on top of her. I began to gently kiss her on her neck, shoulders, and finally on her breast. Once I reached her nipples I was fully erect and began to bite down on each nipple. I could hear her panting and suddenly could feel her grab hold of my cock. Nevaeh began to stroke me as I sucked on her nipples. I then looked up at her and said, "Do you like how that feels in your hands?" She said, "Yes you're bigger than I expected." After a while I slowly pulled away from her and worked my lips to her pelvis. Before going any further I looked back up at her. I could see that she had this surprised look on her face and I just smiled at her.

Without warning I began kissing Nevaeh on her Brazilian waxed pussy lips before parting them with my thumbs. My hands had a firm grip on her inner thighs as they cupped her sweet ass. Play time was officially over and I let my tongue explore Nevaeh's vagina. As my lips and tongue sucked on her plump and juicy clit she began to moan. My dick was harder than a rock and throbbing as I sucked her juices up like a spaghetti noodle.

Before long I had Nevaeh squirming around and making all kinds of loud noises. Once she screamed out that she was about to cum, I worked her clit over until she let it all go. It wasn't too hard to tell that she had an orgasm and it was then that I decided to let her taste her own nectar. I licked all around Nevaeh's lips leaving her juices for her to taste on. I had one hand on my throbbing cock rubbing the tip on Nevaeh's wet pussy lips. Slowly she rose her legs into the air as I penetrated her love canal. Once I was completely inside of her I grabbed hold of her legs. I watched Neicy's face as I throbbed my cock into her pussy repeatedly. I greeted every one of her moans with a heavy sigh. This pussy was good and it wasn't hard to tell that I wasn't enjoying this. It was well worth the wait.

Every time I submerged my dick into your love hole a warm feeling would engulf me. Suddenly I slowed down and watched as I worked my hips causing my cock to slowly enter her from different angles. It came time for us to switch positions being that I had done most of the work. So without warning I stop moving causing Nevaeh to look at me with a confused look on her face. Then as I pulled out slowly and released her legs, I pointed to the chair. "You made me bring that in here for a reason, right?" I said. She looked as if she had forgot about the chair but that look suddenly changed into a look of excitement. It was then that Nevaeh said to me, "Can I tie you up, I mean just your hands?" I looked at her speechless and puzzled for a moment. She went on to say, "I hope you don't think I'm gonna do anything crazy, I just want total control." I finally agreed to being tied up to the chair, it was something I didn't mind doing with her. As she began to tie my hands behind the chair, I could feel her nibbling on my ear.

She was standing behind me which prevented me from seeing her. It was different which made it a suspenseful experience and aroused my interest. Then suddenly in a soft tone Nevaeh was in my ear taunting me. "Would you like my mouth wrapped around your friend there?" Pointing at my dick which began to throb as it hardened before our eyes. All I did was close my eyes and softly respond, "Yes." She started to plant soft kisses on different parts of my body. I could feel her finger softly pressing against my chest moving about. It caused this sensational chill to run through my body. When I finally open my eyes Nevaeh was standing in front of me. The first thing I laid my eyes on was her pussy patch and I was excited because she was about to bounce on my love with it. Next thing I knew she was lifting my head up with her finger under my chin. When eye contact was made Nevaeh was shaking her head from side to side. Then she said, "I don't want you looking down, you need to keep your eyes up here." Instructing me to maintain eye contact, it was as if she enjoyed being in charge. Her words came across seductively demanding and I enjoyed the role she had taken on.

So I did as I was told and locked eyes with her, then she said, "That's more like it, now I'll continue." Nevaeh then sat on the end of my lap not losing eye contact and grabbed hold of my throbbing penis. With this innocent smile on her face she began to jerk me off and with every jerk her grip tighten. It felt extremely good and I could not control my facial expressions. I was moaning, losing control of my jaw as it dropped open. I tried hard to maintain eye contact but my eyes rolled in the back of my head and I glanced at her manhandling my dick. Each time my eyes lost contact with hers. Nevaeh would say, "What did I say about those eyes?" As if I was being a bad boy she stopped jerking me and tighten her grip. It was then that I came to believe that she was a sexual deviant and enjoyed me being tied up. I looked her in the eyes submissively and said, "You told me to keep them on yours at all times." I kind of enjoyed being dominated so didn't mind playing my part. Then without loosening up on my penis, Nevaeh raised up off me and slowly dropped to her knees. As she did so she said remorsefully, "It's ok, I knew it would be hard," while giggling. "I do like how you gave it your best shot," she said. "I'm here to please you and I have no problem doing as I'm told," I said to her as she was kneeling in front of me.

Then I sat and watched with admiration as Nevaeh's eyes made contact with my throbbing, fully erect dick. Stroking it slowly she kissed up the shaft of my cock until she reached the tip. Then as she begun to engulf my dick, she looked up at me. Once she got me inside of her mouth, her tongue went to work as her lips slid up and down my shaft. It felt so good I lost my eyes in the back of my head as I let my head drop back. I moaned and panted as

Nevaeh continued to suck on me like a lollipop. Her warm and moist mouth wrapped around my dick was wonderful feeling. I have to admit being tied up was torture because I couldn't touch her at all.

Still I have to admit it on the other hand the pleasure is intensified. Yet it wasn't long before Nevaeh took my cock out of her mouth then straddled me. Holding my penis with one hand guiding it as she twerked herself on me. Once the head of my penis parted her vaginal lips, she came to a halt. I made eye contact with her and before I knew it her tongue was in my mouth. She started working her hips in a circular motion. Never allowing my penis to enter her completely at the same time not allowing me to be able to push it completely in. It was torture but felt great. YOLO!

Once Nevaeh took her tongue out of my mouth, she watched the facial expression on my face as she completely lowered herself on me. I don't believe she took her eyes off of me as she rode me. I couldn't hold it in and moaned the whole ride until I let my Jiz go inside of her. Even then she continued her ride until she let her cream escape from her sweet pie. It ran down the shaft of my dick onto my leg. It's a one-time experience I will always remember.

Can I Have Some? '06

I had things going pretty good for me, this was my year and I wasn't interested in being committed. Although, I had a good thing going with this female named Leticia, who I let her ride shotgun on the regular. I'll never regret that beautiful summer afternoon when she introduced me to Breanna. Shorty, I messed with was a "G" and pops off if and when it's called for and Breanna wasn't so. Breanna was more of the "I'm too cute to do anything" type. She appeared to be financially stable and far from some hood rat unlike my shorty. Breanna was Puerto Rican and we seemed to bond just because of that alone. I guess that's because I always represent my Puerto Rican half, whether it be the music or the flag in the car.

Breanna had a man, so did shorty but they both were locked up and so they chilled. I won't lie to you I had plotted on Breanna from the first time I laid eyes on her. What made it easier for me was that unlike me Breanna hated driving. So when we use to chill together I always drove. Which put Leticia riding shotgun and Breanna riding in the backseat. I also was aware that Leticia would beat Breanna's ass if she knew about it. It wasn't like I didn't throw hints at Breanna in Spanish but nothing too serious. I use to wonder if that was the reason we always used her vehicle. Breanna always complained about doing the driving and Leticia would suggest that I would drive. Which brought Breanna and me closer together, not to mention we both made money the fast way. So during the day we rip and run the streets and at night we would party hard.

One day when we were out and about I couldn't help but notice Breanna watching me through the rear view. Since I only could exchange looks at red lights I was kind of frustrated that Shorty was around. I didn't want to fuck up what Leticia and I had but I wanted to try my luck with Breanna. After that day I was determined to get Breanna alone and see what was really good. Not really knowing if she and Leticia were truly close or not, I couldn't just be direct about it. Instead I used our line of work to get closed to Breanna. One night at the bar I talked with her about getting some shit from her. Still I refused to just give her my number, just because Leticia was a live wire.

I didn't want Breanna to get beat up or lose what I had going on with Leticia. So to play my cards right I used Leticia to get at Breanna about some work. Being that Shorty wasn't fucking around like that, she wasn't too fond of being the middleman. Then one day I get a call from this unknown number, and come to find out it was Breanna. I first thought it was a set up so I didn't say too much out of the ordinary. She did inform me that Leticia gave her my number so that we didn't involve her in our business deals. Yet, for some strange reason I never tried to stay on the phone with her too long. Before letting her go I told her to call me back with her number unblocked. What I didn't expect was her calling me right back with her number unblocked.

This time she asked, "Listen by the way, do you want to chill one day?" Breanna went on to say, "I Don't really want to drive and Leticia isn't around." "Yeah Leticia took a trip, and I don't mind chillin'," I said. I continued feeling that she might be in over her head with asking me to chill with her while my peoples are out of town. "Are you sure Leticia won't try to flip on you for chillin' wit me?" "Don't worry about it, we won't be driving around in the hood," she said. The way she said it made me smile because the chances of us running into Leticia's friends out of the hood are slim to none. Anyway, I agreed to chill with her but it wasn't going to be that particular day. So we made plans for another day, I told her to just call me. Now little did Leticia know, but I wasn't really in need of Breanna's assistance. Instead it was vice-versa but Leticia wasn't one to divulge that information to everybody.

Breanna was maintaining her image and probably only told me because I was in a position to help. So on the day she called to chill I was caught by surprise. It's not like I heard from her or see her since we last spoke. Now a few days later I'm getting the call, so I had to change my plans. First I had to make up a good excuse for Leticia, which was my P.O. is coming to the crib. She knew I cut my phone off when my P.O. comes through. What was really fucked up is my ex-girlfriend was in town and I told her we would get together that same night. I had promised her any day she choose and that day was the day. Not to mention that I lived with her sister which meant I had to see her.

She never like my line of work but she dealt with it and I knew I was gonna hear it for this one. Out of respect I always tried to be mindful of her feelings toward me. Still it was her fault we weren't together and I found it hard to get back to how we use to be. So it was too hard to blow her off and just deal with her when I get home. All I said was "The streets are calling and I'll try not to be out too late." Afterwards I bounced to my buddy's crib where Breanna came to scoop me up at. When she got there, she asked, "Do you have any thing you have to do first?" As I closed the door to her truck and reclined the seat, I said, "Nah, I took care of everything already, I'm all yours." Before she could even open her mouth I said, "Why you ask?" As she began to pull off she said, "Like you said, you're all mines and the next time you see the hood won't be anytime soon."

I just smiled at her and slowly turned up the radio as we prepared to jump on the highway. I looked at her one more time, lowered the radio and decided to see where her head was at. "So where are we going?" I asked. Breanna said, "I'm going to run a few errands, then whatever." I then said, "You know I can't wait to be alone with you." "I want you to know I am trying to get some of that." Pointing at the pussy. "I thought you and Shorty were serious," she said. "Be for real, you think I look like a Cabrone?" I asked her. "No, but these days you can't be sure, anyway I'm glad because I'm trying to get some," she said glancing between my legs. Breanna went on to say, "I don't know when but hopefully sometime soon." Then I sat back after turning up the radio and enjoyed the ride.

After a few quick stops we grabbed a bite to eat, smoked some weed before heading to her house. I kind of figured she would play hard to get so I decided not to try hard. She said she had a few things to do upstairs and invited me up. Once I got upstairs I did a quick walk through checking out her crib as she picked up around the house. One thing obvious is that she put some nice chance into her apartment. I also notice that the room off of the living room was her closet and the living room area was her bedroom. Which I stood looking out her balcony door admiring the neighborhood, Breanna was picking out an outfit. She felt the need to brag about her large variety of footwear which I showed very little interest.

I went back to looking out the window and asking about the neighborhood, wanting to find a place in an area like hers. She answer my questions and then asked, "What do you think I should wear?" When I turned to see what options she was giving me, I was left speechless. Breanna had took off her clothes, and was standing there in her panties and bra holding two pair of pants in each hand. She had a smirk on her face as she placed the jeans on the side, and sitting on the bed. I walked over to her as I began to unbutton my pants with a smile on my face. I stopped right in front of her and let my pants drop to my ankles as she watched. Breanna looked up at me and said, "Sooner is definitely better than later." As I kicked off my sneakers and stepped out of my pants. "I like sooner a lot better than later," I said. Then I pushed her down onto the bed and climbed on top of her.

Before I knew it my tongue was in her mouth and I was ripping her panties off. Struggling to get them off I got to my knees and yank them off of her. With her nicely shaved pussy in front of me, my dick became rock hard. I then stood up on the bed and let my boxers drop, exposing myself to her. I then dropped back to my knees, then dropping back on top of her. Instead of kissing her on the lips I chose to let my lips and tongue explore her soft flesh. I could hear her moaning as I bit down gently on her hard nipples through her bra. It was then that I decided to go down on her and continued working my way towards her cream pie.

I made a quick stop at her belly button and that's when I felt Breanna position herself on her elbows. When I looked up as I continued to kiss her around her pelvis area. Breanna had this look of disbelief on her face. It was that look on Breanna's face that made me want her even more. I began spreading her legs before I attacked the pussy. One of her legs fell off the bed but I didn't care because it didn't cause any inconvenience. Next I gently began kissing her on her pussy lips before parting them with my tongue. I could feel her squirming and I then used my fingers to part them go my tongue could gain access to her clit. Once Breanna's love bump revealed itself my tongue attacked it causing her to moan heavily. When my tongue went wild on her clit, my fingers invaded her Latin love tunnel.

I savagely sucked and fingered fucked her pussy until she came. Feeling her body squirm uncontrollably I rose to my knees preparing to penetrate her with my erect penis. When at that precise moment she sat up looking past me and grabbed hold of my hard cock. Before I was being submerged into Breanna's mouth. I was still shocked at how fast she went to work on me, like I might disappear right before her eyes. Yet it felt so good and I couldn't help but moan and pant. It wasn't too long before she pulled my dick from in her mouth and slowly began to stroke it. I watched as Breanna did so and when she looked up at me a smile appeared on her face.

I returned her smile and she released my penis as she laid back down. I quickly grabbed both of her legs, placing her feet flat on my chest. Then easing her legs back as I led my penis into Breanna's nicely shaved vagina. I watched as every inch of my cock disappeared into her Latin tunnel. My knees were at the base of her ass, my hands holding her thighs as her feet remained on the outer part of my chest. Once in position I thrust my dick in and out of Breanna's hot and juicy pussy. I fully plunged my dick into her but only pulled it out half way. When I looked up at her, she too watched as I would slow down to enjoy my love muscle penetrate her pussy. To see the faces that she made, I'd pull out all the way making the head of my dick play with her clit. Then I slide it back inside of her and pound it into her pussy.

She moaned loudly and screamed out, "Fuck this pussy Pa, Fuck the shit out of my pussy." Between the sounds Breanna made and the looks on her face, I had no intentions of easing up. It was awhile before I came, and when I was about to bust I pulled out and came all over her pussy. Squeezing out every bit of it all over her as she rolled over onto her stomach. Then she arched her back causing her ass to rise, which in turn caused my penis to stay erect. I was moved by the way Breanna laid there waiting to be penetrated again. As I watched I slowly stroked myself before satisfying her need. Lying flat on top of her, I worked my dick in and out of her. We both moaned and panted to the sounds of my balls slapping her ass. This time when I came it was inside of her as she accepted every bit of me.

I rolled over exhausted but pleased with what had taken place. I was surprised at what extent I went with Breanna. I felt it was well worth it and I had no regrets plus it wasn't nothing wrong with a little foreplay.

For that I said, "Damn Breanna, you were good." Breanna then said, "You damn sure handled your business, does Leticia get the same treatment?" I laughed before saying, "She don't do what you did to bring that out of me, and you actually turned me on without the liquor." Breanna then said, "The way you use your tongue started it and I had to have you in my mouth." She went on to say, "I'm mad this has to end like this." As she got up from the bed I said, "Just call me if you want to get up again, I believe we can work something out." She turned around and walked to my side of the bed and come close to my face and looked me in my eyes that call will come sooner than you think....

The Breakdown

Wow, I was a hot mess during my time of playing the field or rather playing the game. Yes, it was nothing more than game and everyone involved played it to the best of their abilities. The sad truth is that in this game there really isn't any winners or losers, just disappointments. The disappointments come in various forms.

Thinking back now, I suffered my share of them but I handled it like a soldier. I accepted everything that came with the game I played and also learned something from every experience. Still, I was addicted to being promiscuous and due to my selfishness, I played on. From my understanding of the game, I believe I was a great Playa and followed the rules of the game the best.

I never hated on another man or woman regardless of what. Prime example: throw dirt on a man so that I could get with his woman. Yes, I've been that other man in a nice about of relationships.

I never tried to handcuff a woman knowing I was playing the field. Prime example: trying to keep one or every woman I deal with from playing the field, especially not beat on them if I found out there were all the while knowing they had no chance of being my Mrs.

Honestly, there aren't too many women who can say that I even pursued them. In most cases it was the other way around and not because I was a big baller cause that wasn't the case. It's more likely that out the crew I associated with many would say I had the least financially. I guess it was more my swag along with the vibe I gave off that cause me to be fortunate in the game called "Playas."

I accepted each and every female for who they were or portrayed to be. Everyone one judges yet it's yet I didn't allow it to play a factor in how I acted towards them. I was myself with all of them and it didn't matter who I was around nor what the perception was of them. I guess this was another reason I was so fortunate it this game called "Playas." I never viewed as "Playas & Hoes", to me we were all Playa's. The sad truth is that some played the game not really knowing how to play it therefore causing themselves countless disappointments.

In the game of "Playas" the rules don't favor anyone and should not be altered do such. It should always be a fair playing field and if one is fortunate then the disappointment will be next to none and everyone walks away with no ill feelings towards the other gamers and no regrets. There may always be the "What ifs", especially when it comes to the length one chose to stay playing the game.

For me, it wasn't till I ended up in prison that the "What ifs" came into play. Yet, once I was back in the streets that slowly faded to black or not knowing anything other than the game I played for far too long. Being a gamer for as long as I was left very little room for anything real. Too much of anything makes you an addict and my addiction was very bad. The sad truth is that knowing all that I knew about being promiscuous especially the bad still held no weight, which goes to show the level of addiction I had.

Funny thing is that I was motivated by the haters to be the best Playa I could be. The ones who always had something to say about me in any aspect that didn't have respect in front or behind it. I've always considered myself to be a stand-up niggah and maintain a militant outlook so I accepted nothing less from any other niggah. I guess that is one reason why I homered a lot more with females that were in some type of situation which didn't allow for feeling to get twisted.

As you can tell by now, I had a boat load of haters for a dude who wasn't a baller or even a fashion junkie. Can't remember the first or last time I spent over $100 on a shirt or pair of jeans. Never was fond of wearing jewelry and the one set of earrings and watch I did buy, I gave away to my brothers not even a month after buying them. Never even had a ride worth bragging about and the ones I did have were like back dated at least 5 years, lmfao....

I definitely wasn't a movie goer nor did I wine and dine every female I encountered. Percentage wise I would say the 98.7 of the females I encountered didn't see a restaurant or theatre on my expense. Shit the percentage is like 99.1 when it comes to females who even met my family, not relatives and not the family in the streets with me. I'm talking about loved ones, the ones who would never even refer to me by a street name.

There were so many levels to the situationships that partaken in. A few were seasonal, many were the on call or whenever I see you type and the rest were only for the night or weekend. I had a few who caught feelings yet dismissed themselves from the game because they knew I wasn't done playing. I had my share of those who thought they had all the right qualities to make me want to stop playing. I also had those who no matter what they would always allow me to scratch their itch. I can say I probably come in contact with the majority of my situationships in some way and when it does happen most of the time there is always some kind of communication. Whether it be verbally or non-verbal and in some occasions it's to let it be known that it can go down again if only for a night. Nothing I'm bragging about, just stating the facts.

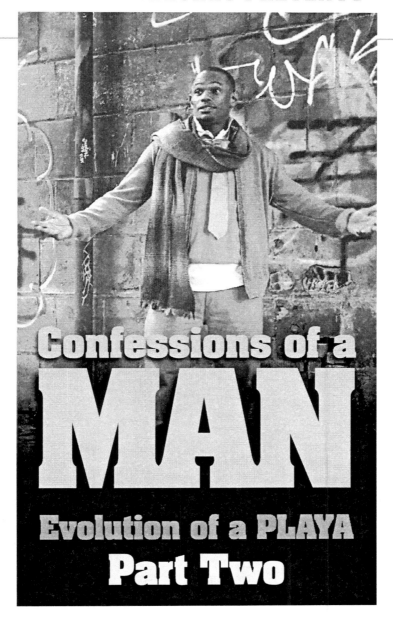

Ready or Not Part Two
'04–'05

The year was ending and a new one was about to begin. so many things were going on in my life and I was confused about my next course of action, when out of the blue my cousin told me she had ran into my old girlfriend. Maritza is her name and I was shocked that she even asked about me. I kind of was surprised when my cousin handed me a number that I could reach Maritza at. I decided not to call her right away, being that I wasn't sure what I would say to her. When I finally called I was sent to her voicemail, so I left a brief message with a number to call me back.

It was later on that evening when I received a phone call from Maritza…

To be continued…

About the Author

I'm from the county of Kings "11207," born and raised. I'm 43 years old and I have two sons, Dominic Christopher Taylor who's 19 years old and who I allowed the streets to rob him of a father, and Jaelin Jermell Gonzalez, who's life is just beginning.

Facing a hefty Federal imprisonment all I could think of was my son Dominic. I was inspired to write so he had a better idea of who his father is mentally and socially. I just felt he should know his father, flaws and all.

This book is the first of many that I put together during my incarceration and I hope they do more than more than just entertain my readers.

LinkedIn: https://www.linkedin.com/in/
   tony-jae-gonzalez-59b668a6

Facebook: https://www.facebook.com/tgonzalezjordan

Twitter: @ajaegonzalez